Motivating Human Service Staff

Supervisory Strategies
for
Maximizing Work Effort
and
Work Enjoyment

Dennis H. Reid
Marsha B. Parsons

Habilitative Management Consultants, Inc.

Published by
Habilitative Management Consultants, Inc.
PO Box 2295
Morganton, North Carolina 28680

ISBN 0-9645562-0-0

Library of Congress Catalog Card Number 95-79661

Printed in the United States of America
10 9 8 7 6 5 4 3 2

DEDICATION

This book is dedicated to those human service supervisors, clinicians, and administrators who spend their work lives trying to ensure the best client services possible by providing a work environment fostering diligence and enjoyment among their staff and colleagues.

ACKNOWLEDGMENTS

We have learned about motivating human service staff from far too many people to acknowledge each person individually. However, several of our supervisors and colleagues have been especially instrumental in teaching us about motivation in the work place. In particular, we thank Jon Bailey and Carolyn Green for their assistance and contributions in research on developing ways of enhancing competence and diligence among human service staff. We also express sincere appreciation to Martin Ivancic, Robert Crow, Robert Schell, Charles Madsen, Iverson Riddle, and Judy Favell for their ideas on how to help people enjoy their work — ideas that have seriously influenced a number of the motivational strategies presented in this book.

CONTENTS

SECTION 1
INTRODUCTION TO MOTIVATION

SECTION 2
ENHANCING DILIGENT AND
COMPETENT WORK PERFORMANCE

SECTION 3
ENHANCING WORK ENJOYMENT

PREFACE

One of the largest and most pervasive industries in the United States is human service delivery. Human service systems exist in every state for people in all age brackets. Treatment and support services are provided through a tremendous variety of human service settings including, for example, preschools, nursing homes, half-way houses, institutions, schools, rest homes, group homes, day treatment centers, and mental health centers.

In order for human service agencies to meet the needs of the clients (consumers) they serve, direct service staff who work in human service agencies must be competent and motivated. Direct service personnel represent the largest segment of the human service work force and have the most contact with agency clients. As such, skilled and hard-working direct service staff are a vital component for quality services. When direct service staff do not know how to perform their jobs proficiently, or do not exert the effort to adequately fulfill their job responsibilities, agency services are seriously hindered. In turn, agency clients do not receive the help they need and seek.

This book presents strategies for enhancing work proficiency and diligence among direct service staff in human service agencies, while ensuring staff enjoy their work. In contrast to typical texts on worker motivation, this book does not focus on theoretical models or interpretations of worker motivation. Rather, the focus is on day-to-day strategies for ensuring staff effectively fulfill their job responsibilities. The strategies are based on decades of applied research on enhancing staff performance in human service settings as well as the supervisory experience of the authors and their colleagues.

The goal of this book is to enable supervisors and related personnel to help their staff work hard and enjoy their work. As will be discussed in the main text, when direct service staff do indeed work hard and enjoy what they do in the work place, agency staff and clients benefit.

The main body of *Motivating Human Service Staff: Maximizing Work Effort and Work Enjoyment* is organized in three interrelated sections. The Introductory section provides a practical, working definition of motivation along with a brief summary of reasons for the widespread existence of motivational problems among human service personnel. The second section, Enhancing Diligent and Competent Work Performance, describes procedures for ensuring staff know how to perform their jobs, and routinely perform their jobs well. The final section, Enhancing Work Enjoyment, details supervisory strategies for increasing the enjoyment staff experience with their day-to-day jobs, while maintaining competent and diligent work habits.

Dennis H. Reid
Marsha B. Parsons

Consumers of human services benefit the most when human service staff are working hard and enjoying their work.

ABOUT THE AUTHORS

Denny Reid and Marsha Parsons have been providing and managing human services for over 20 years. Collectively they have consulted with more than 60 human service agencies in 22 states, and have authored or co-authored three books and four practitioner manuals pertaining to human service provision. With their management friends and colleagues, in 1987 they founded Developmental Disabilities Services Managers, Inc., a nonprofit, international organization designed to enhance the managerial profession in providing human services.

Denny Reid is an experienced clinician, supervisor and administrator. He has been employed as a psychologist in schools and institutions, a residential services director, and an administrator over specialty treatment services in a variety of settings. Denny is also an accomplished applied researcher in the human services, with over 80 journal article and book chapter publications. His work in the human services has resulted in numerous awards, including the North Carolina Department of Human Resources Secretary's Award for Outstanding Service, Western Carolina Center Employee of the Year Award, and the Southeastern American Association on Mental Retardation Richard B. Dillard Award for Research. Denny's current positions include Director of Psychology at Western Carolina Center and Executive Director of Habilitative Management Consultants, Inc. Denny lives with his wife and two sons in Morganton, North Carolina.

Marsha Parsons has experience in a variety of human service roles including classroom teacher, curriculum specialist, school principal, and program consultant. She has published over a dozen applied research articles in human service journals, and serves as editorial consultant for journals and newsletters in the human services. She has been honored as the North Carolina Federation of Business and Professional Women's Outstanding Young Professional Woman, and has also been awarded the Western Carolina Center Association for Retarded Citizens Administrative Award. She is currently the Program Development and Evaluation Specialist at Western Carolina Center and Associate Director of The Carolina Behavior Analysis and Support Center, Ltd. Marsha lives with her husband, son, and daughter in Drexel, North Carolina.

TO CONTACT THE AUTHORS

Denny Reid and Marsha Parsons provide management consultative services to human service agencies and personnel nationwide. Requests for information about services should be directed to them at the address provided below.

Readers are also invited to send comments about this book, as well as suggestions for future editions.

Habilitative Management Consultants, Inc.
P.O. Box 2295
Morganton, North Carolina 28680

SECTION 1

INTRODUCTION TO MOTIVATION

Chapter 1

MOTIVATION: THE ESSENCE OF WORKING HARD AND ENJOYING WORK

One of the most challenging tasks confronting supervisory personnel in human service agencies is staff motivation. Essentially every supervisor faces the situation at some point of supervising staff who are not motivated to perform their duties the way the duties should be performed. When staff are not motivated to fulfill their responsibilities diligently, the services provided to their clients (consumers) are considerably less than optimal, and often neglectful. Inadequate service provision resulting from unmotivated staff has been a problem in every type of human service agency, ranging from preschool centers for toddlers to nursing homes for senior citizens.

Problems resulting from poor motivation and subsequent inadequacies in client services have often reached a crisis state in the recent history of service provision in the United States. To illustrate, inadequate staff performance in state psychiatric and mental retardation facilities has been the focus of numerous law suits brought on behalf of facility clients. The popular press has likewise chastised deficient staff performance, frequently resulting in rather scandalous exposés concerning, for example, the nursing home and child daycare industries. Even public school personnel have been targeted by the media for lack of concern and motivation to effectively teach the nation's children. However, the most consistent indicator of the seriousness of staff motivational problems in the human services exists among the people who must determine means of overcoming such problems—the staff supervisors. We have interacted with hundreds of supervisors around the United States and the most intensely noted problem among supervisors concerning their work is poorly motivated staff.

Although a strong consensus exists among human service supervisors regarding the prevalence of staff motivational problems, agreement does not exist regarding what actually constitutes acceptable motivation. The lack of agreement is not surprising when considering "motivation" historically has been an ambiguous phenomenon in the work world at large, as well as in the human service field. Despite volumes of literature discussing worker motivation in essentially every type of work environment, a consistently agreed upon working definition of motivation has not been readily available. The lack of a working definition is problematic because it is virtually impossible for supervisors to improve staff motivation if supervisors cannot agree on what exactly they are trying to improve.

For the purpose of obtaining high levels of staff motivation in human service settings, motivation is best defined simply as staff persons working hard and enjoying their work. Using this definition, the job of the supervisor for enhancing motivation is to take active steps to ensure staff are working diligently and simultaneously, to take active steps to ensure staff enjoy the work they perform. When supervisors are successful in their efforts to motivate staff in this manner, everybody benefits: the consumers of the agency's services benefit because staff are indeed providing the designated services by working diligently, and the staff benefit because they enjoy what they are doing.

Motivation: Enjoying work
while working hard

Purpose of Motivating Human Service Staff

The purpose of this book is to provide supervisors and related personnel in human service agencies with working strategies for effectively motivating their staff. Using the definition of motivation as just provided, this text presents procedures supervisors can use to:

• Obtain diligent and proficient work performance among staff and,

• Enhance the enjoyment staff experience in their work life.

The procedures to be presented stem from years of applied research on supervisor and staff performance in the work place within the growing field of Organizational Behavior Management (OBM). The basic components of OBM as they relate to motivating staff, and particularly in regard to motivation as just defined, will be discussed in subsequent chapters.

Text Organization

Following introductory comments in this and the subsequent chapter, the remainder of *Motivating Human Service Staff* is organized within two general sections, corresponding to the two components of motivation. The first section, consisting of chapters 3 - 5, focuses on basic OBM procedures for helping staff work diligently and proficiently. The second section, chapters 6 - 10, emphasizes procedures for assisting staff in enjoying their work.

Although the chapters have been categorized into sections for organizational purposes, the procedures discussed in the two sections are quite interrelated. The OBM procedures for promoting diligent work performance presented in the first section, for example, have been selected in light of their general acceptance and likeability among staff. Likewise, those procedures presented in the second section for enhancing staff work enjoyment are discussed only in terms of how the procedures also serve to support supervisory actions for evoking diligent work performance.

Intended Audience

The intended audience of this book is anyone who has supervisory responsibilities for the performance of direct service staff in human service settings. In particular, the primary audience is human service personnel who are employed specifically in a supervisory job. Because many clinicians who are not employed as staff supervisors must solicit the assistance of direct service staff to carry out designated client services, the motivational strategies to be discussed are also relevant for clinical personnel. The motivational procedures are applicable for direct service staff in every type of human service agency, including residential settings such as group homes, nursing homes and state institutions, as well as day treatment settings such as schools, senior centers, preschools, and work activity sites. Although there are of course substantial differences in the work environments of the various types of human service settings, the factors resulting in motivational problems among direct service staff are remarkably similar across each setting.

Due to the focus of this book on motivating paraprofessional, direct service staff, strategies for motivating human service personnel who have professional training and background will not be specifically addressed. Although many of the motivational procedures to be discussed can be applied with professional staff, there are also differences in the job-related characteristics of professional and paraprofessional staff (see Chapter 2) that differentially affect motivational considerations. Relatedly, most of the OBM research upon which much of the content of this book is based, as well as our own experience, has involved paraprofessional, direct service staff. Most importantly however, the focus is on motivating paraprofessional staff because in the vast majority of human service agencies direct service personnel spend the most time with agency clients and have the most significant impact on client well-being. If supervisors can effectively motivate direct service staff then the quality of life among people served by human service agencies is bound to be enhanced.

Before discussing how supervisors can apply OBM procedures to motivate their direct service staff to work hard and enjoy their work, a brief discussion is warranted over why motivation represents such a serious and pervasive problem in the human services. Understanding why motivational problems exist can be helpful in designing effective supervisory strategies for resolving the problems. Chapter 2 provides a brief summary of the roots of motivational problems among staff in typical human service agencies.

Chapter 2

THE ROOTS OF MOTIVATIONAL PROBLEMS

The reasons motivation is often at low levels among staff in human service agencies are many and varied. However, the main reasons can be considered globally within two general categories. The first category is the nature of human service jobs. The second is the nature of the human service work force.

The Nature of Human Service Jobs

A number of features of typical human service jobs result in inherent difficulties in developing and maintaining high levels of staff motivation. Many of the features though can be traced either directly or indirectly to one primary factor: there is not a clear and objective bottom line index of how well a respective human service agency provides its services. The lack of a bottom line measure of agency effectiveness is in stark contrast to most jobs outside of the human service sector. In the former work sector, be it agriculture, business, or industry, a clear bottom line index—the profit margin— guides work place operations. Above and beyond all variables impacting the outcome of any vocational enterprise, the profit margin determines the eventual success or failure of the enterprise. If the profit margin is not satisfactory, the enterprise must change what it is doing or eventually go out of business. In contrast, because the vast majority of human service agencies do not operate on a for-profit basis, there is no profit margin to function as an effectiveness measure.

The lack of one clear and objective bottom-line measure of an agency's effectiveness results in ambiguous determinations regarding how well the agency is functioning. Correspondingly, there are ambiguous determinations of how well the agency's staff are performing. Many human service agencies attempt to provide a measure with which to judge staff effectiveness by generating mission statements describing what the agency is suppose to accomplish. Although mission statements set the occasion for evaluating agency services if clearly developed and disseminated among an agency's staff, mission statements rarely lead to sound evaluations of nonprofit service provision. We challenge the reader to enter any human service agency and ask agency executives to readily show clear and objective measures reflecting how well the agency fulfilled its intended mission during the previous year. Finding such an agency is rare. It is even more uncommon to obtain consistent information from the agency's executive and front line staff about how well the agency has been functioning. Rather, interviews with agency executives and staff will typically result in as many different answers regarding how well or poorly an agency is functioning as the number of staff who are interviewed.

Problems in evaluating staff performance resulting from lack of clear indices of agency effectiveness create a difficult situation for supervisors in terms of staff motivation. The difficulty stems in large part from the confusion often arising over what staff should be doing on a day-to-day basis. Agency staff are frequently provided ambiguous, and even contradictory, direction regarding their priority job duties. Because no bottom line indices exist with which to guide agency operations, executive and/or professional staff typically take the lead in determining what should occur for agency clients and hence, what direct service staff should be doing. However, there is frequent disagreement among administrative and professional staff regarding what constitutes the most important services for agency

clients, and correspondingly, what constitutes the most important duties for staff. Such disagreement exists primarily because
providing human services is by no means an exact science. There
are many different schools of thought across the variety of human service disciplines regarding how to best meet the needs of
people served by human service agencies. The different schools
of thought, or professional orientations, lead to different approaches to providing human services, and different job expectations for staff.

The differing approaches to human service provision represent a long-standing phenomenon, and one that is not likely
to change in the near future. Hence, supervisors should expect
in any human service agency there will be confusion from time
to time over what staff should be doing in the work place. The
confusion must be overcome if supervisors are to effectively
motivate their staff — steps cannot be taken to assist staff in
consistently working hard if it is not clear what the work should
entail. Strategies for overcoming lack of clarity regarding staff
job duties are discussed in Chapter 3. The primary point here is
the nature of human service jobs renders frequent confusion
over how staff should be spending their work time, and such
confusion makes staff motivation problematic.

SUPERVISORS SHOULD BE PREPARED TO OVERCOME DISAGREEMENT AND CONFUSION OVER WHAT CONSTITUTES STAFFS' PRIORITY JOB DUTIES

In addition to difficulties in determining what, and how
well, staff are performing, without bottom line effectiveness
measures it is next to impossible to determine if an agency job
goal has been successfully fulfilled. As a result, the job satisfaction that can occur when staff work individually or together

as a group to achieve a goal is difficult to obtain. What often happens is staff never really experience pride in successfully completing a major agency responsibility. Without a work goal to strive for and achieve, staffs' work requirements become never-ending. Direct service staff become routinized in their work efforts and simply "put their time in" by doing essentially the same thing day after day without working toward, or ever achieving, an apparent goal. The lack of goal-achievement satisfaction disallows one major source of staff motivation in human service agencies that exists in the majority of for-profit businesses: the motivation for staff to work to obtain a goal.

Consequently, by the very nature of many human service agencies, a primary source of job motivation expected in typical work places is lacking from the first day a staff person begins a human service job.

The Nature of The Human Service Work Force

The popular perception of human service personnel typically involves a focus on the traditionally recognized service professions: teachers, psychologists, physicians, social workers, nurses, etc. However, the largest segment of the human service work force does not consist of professional personnel. Most people who work in the human services enter their jobs with no professional preparation for a human service role. The latter individuals — the paraprofessional, direct service work force — typically have an educational history consisting of a high school degree, or a few years of education below or beyond the twelfth grade. Additionally, whereas professional personnel usually are working in a type of job which they chose well before actually beginning the job, direct service staff typically did not begin their jobs based on previous career desires. The latter individuals usually selected a human service job based on immediate economic necessity as well as availability of the job relative to the lack of availability of other types of jobs. Because paraprofessional staff often have chosen their human service job for reasons other than a longstanding desire to perform a particular type of work, they are less likely than professional staff to enjoy their day-to-day work. When staff are not particularly likely to enjoy the work they perform, a significant component of job motivation can be lacking because motivation, as discussed in Chapter 1, entails working hard and enjoying the work.

A second characteristic of the typical work force in many human service agencies having detrimental effects on motivation pertains to the work effort component of motivation, that of working hard. A significant percentage of workers who begin human service jobs do not have good work histories. In some cases the lack of a good work history is simply due to having no prior work experience because the human service job is the first real job for the staff member. As such, the staff person has not had the opportunity to develop diligent work habits. In other cases, new employees in human service agencies have obtained work experience in other jobs, but did not perform effectively in those jobs. The employees typically began their previous jobs in entry level positions, and their job environments did not promote development of diligent work habits sufficient to allow the workers to progress up the career ladder in those occupations. The lack of diligent work habits subsequently carries over to the human service job.

The description of the work force characteristics just presented that make it likely staff motivation will be problematic in human service agencies should be considered carefully. The negative implications regarding motivation should not be considered as a negative commentary on the people themselves who work in human service jobs. On the contrary, the negative implication is many direct service staff have not had the opportunity to work in a motivating environment. Throughout this book a basic contention is when a significant portion of an agency's staff are not motivated as reflected by lack of hard work and/or work enjoyment, the staff are not at fault—the work environment is at fault for not being motivating for staff.

WHEN STAFF ARE NOT MOTIVATED TO PERFORM THEIR JOBS, THE LACK OF MOTIVATION IS DUE TO STAFF WORKING IN AN UNMOTIVATING JOB ENVIRONMENT

Given the premise staff motivation to work diligently is a function of the motivating qualities of an agency's work environment, it follows that a primary component of a supervisor's job is to make the environment conducive for working hard. Further, to ensure staff enjoy their work, the supervisor's job is to find positive rather than negative ways to make the environment supportive of diligent work habits. The differences between positive and negative motivational strategies will be discussed in subsequent chapters. Suffice it to say here that although negative motivational approaches can sometimes result in diligent work performances by staff, or at least temporary diligence, such approaches do not result in staff enjoying their work situation. Because positive motivational strategies result in both diligent work performances over the long term as well as staff enjoyment with their work situation, we will focus on positive means of motivating staff.

A PRIMARY COMPONENT OF A SUPERVISOR'S JOB IS TO FIND POSITIVE MEANS OF MAKING THE WORK ENVIRONMENT MOTIVATING

The contention that it is the supervisor's responsibility to motivate staff by using positive strategies is not a universally popular concept, and particularly among some working supervisors. Many supervisors believe staff should be inherently motivated to perform their responsibilities diligently. In actuality, many staff in human service agencies are extremely motivated to work regardless of their surrounding work environment. It is well known in management circles the best way to have a group of hard working staff is to hire people who are internally motivated to be diligent workers.

We agree with the concept of hiring internally motivated staff to work in the human services. However, highly motivated staff are not always available when employment opportunities arise. Also, sometimes staff who are thought to be internally motivated to work diligently do not turn out to be hard workers when they begin their human service jobs. Relatedly, staff may be highly motivated when they begin their jobs but because their daily work environment is not highly motivating, the staff soon lose their motivation. Anyone who has worked in the human services very long has witnessed the sad situation of new employees beginning their jobs with considerable motivation and then gradually losing the desire to work hard. As discussed in subsequent chapters, the loss of work motivation is due in many agencies to management actions placing staff in unpleasant situations that compete against staff feeling good about the work place. In other agencies, new and highly motivated employees are chastised by older, more experienced staff. The latter individuals do not appreciate the new employees' diligent work habits because the diligent work makes the more experienced yet less motivated staff look bad. New employees eventually respond to the resentment from more experienced staff by reducing their work efforts.

As just indicated, the belief staff should be inherently motivated, and a supervisor should not have to motivate staff, is often erroneous when examining situations existing in human service agencies. There is also another common belief about staff motivation in the human services that is often inaccurate when considering how agencies typically operate. Specifically, a popular notion among the public at large is people who work in the human services have a unique quality for patience and caring for people in need of support — a quality presumed to motivate human service staff to perform their jobs diligently. Many readers have undoubtedly heard this view expressed in social interactions when the readers have attempted to describe the type of work they perform to people who do not work in human services. When explaining one's human service job to someone unfamiliar with the human services, a typical response is the human service worker must have alot of patience and be a special kind of person to perform such work.

The degree to which the popularly viewed qualities of human service workers actually exists is unclear. We certainly hope the view is true for the majority of staff in the human services, and fully believe a caring attitude for clients is a priority criterion when considering whom to employ in human service jobs. However, our experience as well as numerous research findings clearly indicate a patient and caring concern for people in need, when and where it exists, does not ensure staff maintain high levels of work motivation on a day-to-day job basis. The fact that staff motivation is such a pervasive problem in the human services attests to the difficulties in simply relying on staffs' concern for others to consistently motivate staff to work diligently and proficiently.

The reasons why concern for helping people in need, be they people with mental, psychiatric, educational, or physical disabilities, frequently does not serve to sufficiently motivate human service staff are complex. Many of the reasons should become apparent upon reading the remainder of this text. At this point suffice it to say the way many human service agencies operate actually discourages staffs' concern for others functioning as a day-to-day job motivator for staff. To illustrate, many of the decisions significantly affecting the quality of life of clients served by human service agencies are not made by direct service staff but by senior agency executives. At times staff are not in agreement with the executive decisions because staff believe the decisions are not in the best interest of client welfare. Consequently, direct service staff quickly realize executive decisions can occur that have significant impact on client welfare regardless of what the staff themselves are doing.

Such awareness in turn causes staff to realize their hard work in and of itself will not guarantee fulfillment of their desire to meet the needs of their clients. As a result, staffs' concern for client welfare becomes insufficient for motivating staff to work hard on a daily basis — staff know managerial actions may totally negate their work efforts to enhance client well being.

In short, regardless of whether staff should be highly motivated, often they are not. It is the supervisor's responsibility to help staff become motivated, and stay motivated. If the supervisor chooses not to accept the responsibility to motivate staff, or does not know how to positively motivate, then the supervisor must contend with the undesirable situations noted in Chapter 1 that result when human service staff are poorly motivated to perform their jobs.

SECTION 2

ENHANCING DILIGENT AND COMPETENT
WORK PERFORMANCE

Chapter 3

ENHANCING STAFF WORK EFFORT: PINPOINTING AND MONITORING STAFF PERFORMANCE

In Chapter 1, motivation was defined as involving two components: working hard and enjoying work. This chapter focuses on the work component — the degree to which staff are serving clients in a diligent and competent manner. If staff are not working diligently and competently, attention must be directed toward improving the quantity and quality of their work.

The reasons why many direct service staff in human service agencies lack diligent work habits were discussed in Chapter 2. Regardless of the reasons for poor work habits however, supervisors are still responsible for staffs' work performance. When staff performance is indeed inadequate, a primary job of a supervisor is to change staffs' work behavior. Equally importantly, when staff job performance is adequate, a supervisor's job is to maintain the performance. Despite the myriad of job duties supervisors are expected to perform, improving their staffs' work performance and maintaining the improvements is the most critical supervisory function in a human service agency.

THE PRIMARY COMPONENT OF A SUPERVISOR'S JOB IS TO CHANGE INADEQUATE STAFF PERFORMANCE AND MAINTAIN ADEQUATE PERFORMANCE

Ensuring staff are working diligently to provide the best possible client services is no easy task for many supervisors.

The characteristics of both the work force and the nature of human service jobs as discussed in Chapter 2 can present numerous obstacles to effective job performance. Nevertheless, successful supervisors promote diligence and competence among their staff despite the inherent obstacles. The latter supervisors are successful in large part because they possess specific skills for changing problematic staff performance and maintaining desirable performance. However, not all human service supervisors have the necessary work skills to be successful in this regard.

The lack of effective supervisory skills among certain supervisors should come as no surprise to individuals familiar with the operations of typical human service agencies. When initially hired, human service supervisors are unlikely to have any preservice training in how to supervise. Many supervisors are promoted from the ranks of direct service providers (e.g., teachers, social workers, nurses, primary care workers) because of their competent performance in those roles. Competent performance in a direct service or clinical role though does not guarantee competent performance as a supervisor. Accomplishing work through others, which is the essence of supervision, requires different skills than the skills necessary to perform direct service work oneself. Few human service supervisors possess the former set of skills when initially assuming a supervisory position.

Compounding the lack of effective supervisory skills among new supervisors is the fact that inservice training in supervision provided by most human service agencies is weak at best. Often, when agencies provide inservice training in supervision the training is more theoretical than practical, consisting of more flash than substance. To illustrate, at a recent workshop we attended on staff supervision, the workshop leader encouraged attendees to identify their supervision style by selecting answers to a series of questions about personal habits and preferences. When numerical values for selected answers were summed, the respective scores indicated a set of personality traits (e.g., thorough, factual and reserve or social, risk-taker and idealistic). Knowledge of personality type was reported to enhance supervisory ability. In actuality though, while such introspective analysis about one's personality can be interesting, it rarely results in information directly assisting supervisors in resolving staff performance problems. Unless inservice training equips supervisors with specific skills for resolving staff performance problems encountered on the routine job, the utility of the inservice training is questionable.

One approach to supervision which provides supervisors with practical solutions to staff performance problems is Organizational Behavior Management (OBM). An OBM approach to supervision can be summarized as a series of active supervisory steps for enhancing staff performance in the work place. As noted in Chapter 1, years of applied research in business and human service settings have shown that consistent application of OBM procedures effectively resolves a wide variety of staff performance problems. Noted performance problems resolved through OBM strategies have included, for example, absenteeism, nonproficient administrative performance, ineffective client-teaching skills, unsafe work practices, lack of therapeutic client interactions, excessive time spent in nonwork activities, and inadequate healthcare provision.

In addition to effectiveness in resolving staff performance problems, several other characteristics make OBM particularly useful as a supervisory strategy. First, an OBM approach is performance-oriented in that the focus of supervision is on what staff do when at work. In this regard, it is what staff actually do with and for agency clients that determines whether or not an agency provides a satisfactory quality of service. Hence, supervisors must be able to impact what staff do in the work place on a day-to-day basis. Second, an OBM approach is technological; supervisory approaches are presented as specific techniques, allowing supervisors with no educational background in supervision to know what to do to resolve a variety of staff performance problems. Because OBM emphasizes primarily positive supervisory procedures, OBM strategies are also acceptable to staff. Staff satisfaction due to acceptance of supervision is an essential component of a motivating work environment.

In summary, using an OBM model as a blueprint for effective supervision is highly recommended because OBM procedures are effective, performance-oriented, technological, and acceptable. The basic steps comprising an OBM approach to supervision can be briefly summarized as:

1. Pinpoint staff work performance that needs to be changed or maintained.
2. Monitor staff performance in order to obtain information used in management decision-making.
3. Train skills staff need to accomplish the work if staff lack necessary work skills.
4. Provide positive consequences to increase desirable work performance.

Although the steps in an OBM approach to supervision can be succinctly stated as just indicated, the actual application of the steps to different staff performance areas can be much more varied and complex. The purpose of this chapter is to begin describing OBM steps in terms of specific strategies which set the occasion for diligent and proficient work performance. Specifically, this chapter discusses procedures involved in the first two OBM steps: delineating staff performance expectations and monitoring staff performance. Subsequently, Chapter 4 discusses the third OBM step, focusing on training necessary work skills to staff for meeting performance expectations. The last chapter in the first section of this book, Chapter 5, summarizes application of consequence procedures for actually improving and maintaining diligent work habits. Consistent application of the strategies summarized in Chapters 3 to 5 will help fulfill the first component of a supervisor's staff motivation responsibility, that of ensuring staff work hard on a day-to-day basis.

Pinpointing Work Performance

Before staff can be expected to work diligently and competently, they must have a clear understanding of exactly what is expected of them. Ensuring staff are fully aware of job expectations is frequently more difficult than many supervisors realize. Supervisors often assume staff will know what is expected of them without much explanation. Such an assumption is usually erroneous when considering the nature of the work performed by direct service staff. Direct service staff in essentially every human service agency are required to perform a wide array of different jobs everyday. To illustrate, a staff person in a preschool program is typically responsible for the cleanliness, safety and stimulation of the children in the preschool while simultaneously being responsible for completion of required paperwork, interaction with parents and maintenance of the environment. Similarly, a direct service person in a group home for children with behavior disorders must teach appropriate social behavior while protecting children from their own aggressive behavior or the behavior of other children. The same staff must interface treatment strategies practiced in the group home with those of the child's family members, school and clinical staff. Given all of these competing responsibilities, which specific duty is most important to perform at any point in time is not always readily apparent to staff.

In addition to the varied nature of direct service work, a reason staff are not always aware of job expectations is the actual work involved in fulfilling a job responsibility may not be obvious. For example, it may not be evident exactly what a supervisor means when she instructs staff to "provide leisure activities" for clients. To the staff, providing a leisure activity may mean giving each client something to do by simply handing each client a leisure material. In contrast, to the supervisor, providing a leisure activity may mean organizing a group activity, actively assisting each client to participate in the activity, and routinely changing the activity every 30 minutes or so.

Because the job of direct service staff is varied and sometimes ambiguous, how supervisors inform staff about expected work responsibilities deserves careful consideration. In particular, performance expectations must be well specified for staff. Specification of job duties can be accomplished in a number of ways. Sometimes performance expectations can be specified using only simple verbal descriptions whereas for other duties, much more verbal as well as written detail is required. Regardless of the simplicity or detail, all descriptions of performance expectations should share three characteristics. Supervisors should describe performance expectations in terms of specific, observable, and measurable work behaviors.

In conducting training workshops with supervisors around the country, we have found describing staff work duties in very specific terms to be difficult for many supervisors. There seems to be a natural tendency to describe performance problems as broad generalizations, often reflecting a supervisor's opinion of a staff person's overall work style in contrast to specific work behaviors. Telling a staff person who is completing an insufficient amount of work, for example, "to take more initiative with her work" does little to specify what duties the supervisor actually expects of the employee. On the other hand, providing the employee with a list of specific jobs expected to be completed each day provides the employee with a more clear directive for her performance. Similarly, a general instruction to staff to "keep the group home clean" may not result in an acceptably clean home because the instruction is not specific enough to delineate exactly what cleaning activities should be completed. In short, in order to ensure work expectations are clear to staff, expected job duties must be described in terms of specific work behaviors.

TO ENSURE STAFF ARE FULLY AWARE OF WHAT IS EXPECTED OF THEM, PERFORMANCE EXPECTATIONS MUST BE PROVIDED IN TERMS OF JOB DUTIES THAT ARE SPECIFIC, OBSERVABLE, AND MEASURABLE

Equally important as describing job expectations as specific work behaviors, job duties must be presented in observable and measurable terms. Neither the work itself nor the outcome of work performance can be described sufficiently when supervisors express performance expectations using general descriptors such as understands, cooperates, recognizes, thinks, or knows. When work cannot be specifically observed or quantified, the quality of the work is open to question because one cannot directly verify the work has occurred, or occurred satisfactorily. In contrast, when general and unobservable descriptors of work such as understands, cooperates, recognizes, etc., are translated into clearly defined, observable work behaviors, work accomplishment can be readily verified.

The process of refining broad generalizations concerning staff work performance into specific, observable and measurable descriptions of work is called performance pinpointing. To illustrate the concept of pinpointing, the reáder should consider a situation in which a school principal is concerned about a teacher's assistant who displays a negative attitude when interacting with students. Rather than advising the assistant to improve her negative attitude, the school principal should pinpoint specific behaviors which the assistant should perform — behaviors that can be seen and measured. The assistant could be instructed, for example, to provide more frequent interactions denoting approval such as smiling at students, patting them on the back, and praising the things done correctly, and less frequent interactions denoting disapproval such as describing something done wrong, reprimanding or frowning. When negative and positive attitudes are translated into specific work behaviors, the assistant will have a better idea of her job expectations. Relatedly, during future visits to the classroom the principal can more readily and objectively observe for a more positive attitude on the part of the assistant.

Performance Pinpointing Using Task Analyses

Some work activities require more structure or elaboration than can be accomplished with a specific statement or two as represented in the illustration just noted. In particular, more elaboration is usually needed when a staff member must perform several activities in sequence to complete a complex work activity. Complex work tasks can be appropriately pinpointed for staff by delineating in a step-by-step fashion exactly what staff should do to complete the tasks. When work activities are broken down into a series of more simple actions or steps, the result is a job task analysis. To illustrate, in order for nursing home staff to safely lift nonambulatory individuals to move them from their wheelchairs to their beds, staff must engage in a series of actions. If the actions are performed incorrectly staff risk serious injury to themselves and their clients. In order to make the correct lifting method explicit for staff, the lifting process can be task analyzed as exemplified below.

EXAMPLE OF A TASK ANALYSIS OF A STAFF JOB DUTY

Lifting and Transferring People Who are Nonambulatory

1. Lock wheels of wheelchair
2. Stand next to chair with feet apart about shoulder width
3. Place one arm under client to support head and neck
4. Place other arm under client between hips and knees
5. Keep back straight and contract stomach muscles
6. Lift and transfer keeping client's weight close to body

For rather complex or potentially dangerous work tasks such as lifting, all steps in the task analysis should be performed in the listed sequence. For other complex work activities, performing steps in an exact sequence may be unimportant as long as all steps in the task analysis are completed. For instance, the procedures for taking preschoolers on a field trip could be broken down into a series of actions to be completed, although it may not be necessary to complete the actions in any particular sequence (e.g., obtaining parental permission, securing a vehicle and driver, signing for medications, notifying appropriate people). It is the supervisor's responsibility to determine which specific job tasks have to be completed in a certain sequence by staff. The primary point is complex job expectations of staff should be presented as specific actions using task analyses. Numerous job duties, such as giving medications, responding to emergencies, conducting client teaching sessions, and cleaning items contaminated with body fluids represent complex, multistep work activities common in human service agencies that can be clearly described for staff through task analyses.

Performance Pinpointing Using Activity Schedules

Another method for defining staff work expectations familiar to many human service supervisors is an activity schedule. Activity schedules represent written assignments that structure the work routine for individual staff or for groups of staff. Although activity schedules are utilized in many agencies including nursing homes, group homes, and institutions, we have found schedules are often inadequately structured for effective pinpointing of staff job expectations. For activity schedules to be useful in clarifying performance responsibilities, schedules should be explicit enough to communicate to a staff member when, where, with what and with whom the staff person should be working. Likewise, schedules should contain sufficient detail to allow a supervisor to locate a staff person and quickly determine if the staff member is performing appropriate duties based on the scheduled activities. To illustrate, Schedule 1 presented on the following page represents an excerpt from an activity schedule that is common in many child day care centers. Schedule 1 is far too vague to be of much assistance in clarifying staff performance responsibilities. In contrast, Schedule 2 specifies when, where, with what and with whom staff should be working. Based on Schedule 2, not only will staff have a clear understanding of the expected work, a supervisor could quickly observe whether a given staff member is in the appropriate location and conducting the job activity specified by the schedule.

EXAMPLE OF ACTIVITY SCHEDULES
FOR A DAY CARE ROUTINE

Schedule 1	
8:30 - 10:00	All staff and students rotate through water, table games and music center activity.

Schedule 2

Time	Staff	Children	Activity
8:30 - 9:00	Sue	Billie, Mary, Ted, Sue	Water table
	Camille	John, Ellen, Leslie, Cliff	Table game, Color Bingo
9:00 - 9.30	Groups switch activities		
9:30 - 9:45	Sue	All children	Music center, use instruments
	Camille		Break
9:45 - 10:00	Staff switch activities		

Performance Pinpointing Through Goal Setting

Once performance expectations are stated in terms of specific, observable and measurable behaviors, work expectations can be further pinpointed by setting performance goals (see Chapters 6 and 9 for how goal setting can also enhance staff enjoyment in the work place). Performance goals specify an expected, satisfactory level of work performance. When considering, for example, the teacher's assistant whose interactions with students seem too negative as described earlier, desirable interactions (interactions denoting approval such as telling the student what he did correctly, patting him on the back, smiling) and undesirable interactions (interactions denoting disapproval such as telling the student what he did wrong, reprimanding, frowning) were defined. To set a performance goal, the amount of positive and negative interactions for which the assistant should strive could be specified by the principal. The principal might determine an appropriate goal would be engaging in four times as many positive interactions with the student as negative interactions. Subsequent observations of the assistant's interactions would reveal whether her work behavior is in line with the established performance goal.

To exemplify further the process of setting performance goals, the following pairs of statements regarding staff performance problems should be contrasted. The first statement reflects a very general description of a performance problem. The second description demonstrates how the performance problem can be presented as a specific, observable and measurable performance goal.

EXAMPLES OF PERFORMANCE STATEMENTS DEPICTING VAGUELY STATED WORK PROBLEMS (A) AND APPROPRIATELY STATED, SPECIFIC PERFORMANCE GOALS (B)

EXAMPLE 1

A. Jane is always late with paperwork.

B. Jane's progress notes will be in the client's record by the 15th of each month and client evaluations will be on the supervisor's desk by one week before the team planning meeting.

EXAMPLE 2

A. Jack, the vocational director, needs to expand his program by securing more jobs for clients in the community.

B. By this time next year, ten clients currently working in the sheltered workshop will have jobs at community businesses.

EXAMPLE 3

A. Joe, the school guidance counselor, spends too much time in his office and not enough time getting to know the students.

B. Joe will spend at least one hour in every classroom each month.

EXAMPLE 4

A. The clients with multiple disabilities who live at Riverside Group Home spend their leisure time with nothing to do.

B. During leisure times at least 80% of the clients will have a leisure material within arm's reach and 80% will receive either a prompt or reinforcer for engaging with the material during a 5-minute observation period.

Determining Work Activities To Pinpoint

At this point, it probably has become apparent performance pinpointing can be a time-consuming process. Considering the time involved in pinpointing work responsibilities and the varied array of work duties required of direct service staff, it quickly becomes evident pinpointing all work duties would be essentially impossible. Hence, supervisors should consider the total set of work duties required of staff and determine which work activities warrant the investment of time and effort required for pinpointing. We offer two guidelines to assist in selecting which work responsibilities to pinpoint. First, consideration should be given to those work activities directly relating to achieving the primary mission of the agency. If the primary agency mission is to increase client independent functioning, for example, then work duties pertaining to instructional or habilitative activities should be pinpointed. Alternatively, if the primary mission of the agency is to provide health care and safety, then job duties associated with medical and personal care as well as general client supervision should be considered for pinpointing.

A second guideline for determining which job duties to pinpoint is to consider aspects of staff performance that interfere with achieving the agency's primary mission. This guideline emphasizes the importance of pinpointing undesirable staff work habits obstructing the smooth operation of an agency such as excessive absenteeism, tardiness, staff bickering among themselves, or frequent complaining about a supervisor's directives. Once the unwanted staff activities are explicitly pinpointed, as well as more appropriate staff behaviors, then the OBM steps as described later in this and subsequent chapters for improving staff performance can be effectively implemented.

Monitoring Staff Performance

After performance goals have been pinpointed, the next step in an OBM approach to supervision is to monitor staff performance. Monitoring involves systematically collecting objective information indicative of how well or how poorly staff are completing the previously defined work duties.

Many supervisors are not aware systematic monitoring of staff performance is a critical component of effective supervision. As a result, information regarding staff performance is obtained unsystematically by monitoring staff performance on an infrequent, inconsistent or haphazard basis. At times, supervisors avoid monitoring staff performance altogether.

When supervisors do monitor staff work activities systematically, almost without exception staff report they dislike having their performance monitored. Staffs' negative reactions to having their performance monitored in turn causes many supervisors themselves to seriously dislike monitoring. Nevertheless, having an accurate, objective evaluation of staff performance is essential to providing effective supervision. Without objective information derived from systematic monitoring, supervisors will not know when to implement procedures to change or to maintain aspects of staffs' job performance. Supervisors must determine what monitoring procedures are best suited for measuring different aspects of staff performance and how staffs' negative reaction to monitoring can be reduced.

Before discussing specific procedures for monitoring staff performance and increasing staff acceptance of performance monitoring, two general guidelines warrant mentioning that are applicable to staff monitoring regardless of the procedures utilized. First, supervisors should obtain information regarding a staff member's performance by directly observing either the staff member's work or work outcome. Although supervisors may be tempted to formulate opinions of a staff person's performance indirectly based on reports from other agency staff (e.g., the staff person's co-workers, other supervisors or even the supervisor's supervisor), the other staff may have different performance expectations than the staff person's supervisor. Moreover, other agency staff may not be sufficiently familiar with the specific work situation to fairly evaluate the staff person's performance. In some cases, an individual may unjustly describe a staff person's performance in an undesirable light simply because the individual does not like the staff person or is jealous of him. Basing supervisory decisions on second hand reports about staff performance can cause much disgruntlement among staff who question the objectivity of, and motivation for, such decisions.

A second guideline for performance monitoring is to monitor consistently so each time a particular work activity is observed, the monitoring process is the same. When inconsistency exists in what work behaviors are measured or how the behaviors are monitored, any variability observed with staffs' performance may be the result of the inconsistent monitoring method and not be indicative of true changes in performance. To illustrate, when observing a teacher's classroom management skills, a principal may initially measure student on-task behavior by counting children who are appropriately using educational materials. During the next observation the principal may count the children who are using educational materials in any way regardless of whether the students are using the materials appropriately. Consequently, the teacher's performance in terms of keeping students on task may appear to improve from the first observation to the second when in actuality, the difference in performance measures may have been due solely to the inconsistent monitoring procedure.

Consistency in monitoring is especially important when the effects of supervisory actions intended to improve staff performance are being evaluated. In the example just described, the principal may have had a talk with the teacher after the first observation concerning the importance of keeping students on task. The effects of the principal's talk on the teacher's subsequent performance could not be accurately evaluated unless the teacher's performance was monitored in the same way during each of the principal's classroom observations. Monitoring consistency can be enhanced by ensuring performance is pinpointed and monitoring procedures are implemented uniformly across repeated observations of the pinpointed performance.

The best method for monitoring staff performance will depend on characteristics of the work behaviors to be monitored as well as what procedures are most convenient for the supervisor. Although an infinite array of monitoring strategies can be designed, only those monitoring methods typically found most applicable to evaluating staff performance in human service agencies will be discussed. For more in-depth information on methods of monitoring and measuring staff performance, see Selected Readings.

MONITORING SHOULD INVOLVE DIRECT OBSERVATION OF STAFFS' WORK OR WORK OUTCOME AND BE CONDUCTED IN A CONSISTENT MANNER

Event Recording

Sometimes supervisors keep a record of the number of times a work activity or performance problem occurs by counting every occurrence of the work behavior. Measuring staff performance by counting each occurrence of a designated work behavior can be useful when the work occurs relatively infrequently and can be counted as a discrete event (i.e., has a definite beginning and end). A familiar example of event recording is a staff person's work attendance record. When an employee calls in sick, a record is made of the absence such that each absence can be counted and totaled on a monthly or annual basis. Similar recording procedures can be useful for monitoring the frequency of discrete events such as back injuries, reports of client mistreatment, client treatment goals achieved, medication errors, or staff attendance at inservice training sessions. Event recording produces an accurate measure of how often a particular work activity or problem occurs. Presented below is an example of an event recording sheet used to monitor the cancellation of therapeutic service sessions in a day program for people with severe disabilities.

SAMPLE EVENT RECORDING SHEET FOR MONITORING CANCELLATION OF CLIENT TREATMENT SERVICES

Cancellation of service record for month of May, 1995				
Date	Client	Service Cancelled	Responsible Person	Reason for Cancellation
5/8/95	Sue	P.T	Ann	Staff illness
5/10/95	Fred	Speech	Lisa	Staff meeting
5/16/95	Troy	O.T.	Mike	Staff illness
5/17/95	Fred	Speech	Lisa	Staff meeting

One disadvantage of event recording as a performance monitoring procedure is it is impractical for measuring some types of work activities. Recording every behavioral occurrence would be close to impossible for work behaviors which happen on a very frequent basis. For example, a residential supervisor may be concerned clients are receiving an inadequate number of positive interactions from direct service staff. Expecting a supervisor to count each occurrence of a positive interaction throughout the entire work day would be rather ludicrous. Work activities occurring on a frequent basis can be evaluated much more easily using time-sampling techniques.

Time-Sampling Procedures

Time sampling involves making brief yet systematic observations during a portion of the time in which a work activity is expected to occur. After several observations, the pattern of work observed during the frequent, brief samples becomes representative of a staff person's overall pattern of work. To illustrate, if a nursing home supervisor wants to increase residents' choice opportunities during leisure activities, observations could be conducted for 10 minutes of the designated leisure time on several days. During the observations the number of times staff provide residents with a choice of leisure activities could be recorded. After conducting several 10-minute observations during the scheduled leisure time across a few days, a supervisor will have a good idea regarding the approximate number of choices typically offered during leisure time. A simple form for recording leisure choices during a 10-minute observation period is presented on the following page. During each minute of the observation, the number of choice presentations provided by staff and the number of choices made by residents are recorded.

EXAMPLE OF A TIME-SAMPLING SYSTEM
FOR MONITORING AMOUNT OFCHOICES
DURING LEISURE TIME

Date: _3/8/95_   Time: _2:15_   Location: _Game Room_
Staff: _Alice Harper_   Residents: _Mr. Block, Ms. Becker, Ms. Marshall_

Minute	Staff choice presentations	Resident choices
1	_Mr. Block, magazine/music_	magazine
2		
3		
4	_Mr. Marshall, magazine/music_	_no choice_
5		
6	_Ms. Becker, jewelry/painting_	_jewelry making_
7	_Ms. Marshall, jewelry/painting_	_jewelry making_
8		
9		
10		

Total number: presentations _4_   choices _3_

Time-sampling techniques are particularly useful when the work performance of concern is essentially continuous, or extends throughout a large portion of the work day. Staff compliance with activity schedules represents one type of work responsibility expected to occur on a continuous basis throughout the day. To accurately evaluate work extending over much of the work day such as schedule compliance, frequent yet brief observations can be made at various intervals during the day. The observations can be conducted on a formal basis by establishing a specific schedule of times to observe staff performance each week. Time sample observations can also be conducted more informally, during occasions when the supervisor happens to be walking through the staff work area and makes brief notes regarding what staff are doing. A format for implementing a time sample system for monitoring staff compliance with an activity schedule is presented below.

EXAMPLE OF A TIME-SAMPLE FORM FOR MONITORING STAFF COMPLIANCE WITH A WORK ACTIVITY SCHEDULE

Date: *3/6/95*   Y = yes   N = no

Observation

1. Time	8:20 am	Staff	Jim S.	On schedule?	~~Y~~	N
2. Time	11.00 am	Staff	Sara D.	On schedule?	~~Y~~	N
3. Time	12:15 pm	Staff	Jim S.	On schedule?	Y	~~N~~
4. Time	3:00 pm	Staff	Jim S.	On schedule?	Y	~~N~~
5. Time	3:20 pm	Staff	Sara D.	On schedule?	~~Y~~	N

When using time-sample monitoring procedures, a number of observations of staff performance must be obtained for the resulting information to be representative of an employee's routine performance. No supervisory action should be based on only one or two observations because each observation represents a small sample of the employee's overall performance. Basing management decisions on insufficient information regarding employee performance can often lead supervisors to react in error which in turn, can be a source of considerable staff dissatisfaction in the work place. For example, a supervisor who visits a staff member on only two occasions, observes the staff person taking a break on both occasions, and concludes the staff member is not a hard worker, is likely making an erroneous conclusion. The observations may have occurred during the only breaks the staff person took all day such that the observed performance is not representative of the staff person's routine performance. In contrast, if the supervisor visits the staff member frequently at different times during the week and usually finds the staff member taking a break, the resulting impression is more likely to be an accurate representation of routine performance and can become the basis for appropriate corrective action by the supervisor.

The major advantage of using time-sampling techniques to monitor staff performance is time efficiency. Typically, time-sampling procedures require only a few minutes of the supervisor's time to complete. Because the types of work performance amenable to monitoring through time-sampling occur frequently or over relatively long periods of time, observations can be scheduled essentially at the supervisor's convenience as noted earlier. Relatedly, because time samples involve brief observations, they can often be conducted at the same time as other supervisory duties. To illustrate, when entering the work area to give a staff member a telephone message, a supervisor could quickly observe each staff member's activity, make a mental note regarding what staff are doing, and then record the information upon returning to the office.

Performance Checklists

An accurate evaluation of some types of work activities is difficult to accomplish during quick, periodic observations such as those used in time sampling. When work activities must be observed from beginning to end to obtain an accurate evaluation of a staff member's performance, checklists can be useful monitoring tools. A performance checklist is simply a task analysis (see previous discussion of task analysis in this chapter) which includes a succinct description of all steps a staff person must perform to complete a respective work task satisfactorily. As a staff member engages in the work activity, each step on the checklist can be marked by the supervisor as completed either correctly or incorrectly by the staff member. Performance checklists are convenient monitoring tools when work accuracy or detail is more of a concern than frequency of occurrence.

An example of a work activity conducive to monitoring with a performance checklist exists in residential settings serving clients who have severe developmental disabilities. In these settings, supervisors are often responsible for direct service staffs' implementation of programs designed to teach clients adaptive skills. When observing a client-teaching session conducted by a staff member, the supervisor could use the following checklist to monitor the proficiency of staffs' client-teaching performance.

EXAMPLE OF A PERFORMANCE CHECKLIST FOR
MONITORING STAFF TEACHING SKILLS WITH CLIENTS
WHO HAVE SEVERE DEVELOPMENTAL DISABILITIES

Staff name _Markus Kirk_ Date _4/3/95_ Location _classroom_
Client name _Dan Rowe_   Skill to be taught _playing tape player_

		Yes	No
1	Staff trains all steps in the client program in corect order.	✓	
2	When more than one teaching prompt is required on a single program step, staff follows a least-to-most assistive prompting sequence.	✓	
3	Staff reinforces client behavior only when the client completes a step correctly.	✓	
4	Staff always reinforces the client after the last completed step of the skill.	✓	
5	If the client makes an error, staff stops the client and has the client repeat the incorrectly completed step while giving a stronger prompt than on the previous trial.		✓

Using checklists to monitor staff performance as just illustrated presents several advantages for supervisors. In particular, because all necessary steps for completing the task are listed in a brief format, the checklist serves as a nice reminder for the supervisor regarding the critical steps to evaluate when observing staffs' performance. Relatedly, when supervisors are discussing results of the monitoring with staff, a checklist can serve as a convenient guide for the discussion. A checklist can likewise be given to staff following the monitoring session as a written reminder of what aspects of the staff person's performance should be most carefully attended to in future work.

Permanent Product Monitoring

The types of monitoring procedures most familiar to supervisors are usually those involving permanent products resulting from certain work activities. In permanent product monitoring systems, the product or outcome of staffs' work rather than the work activity per se is the basis for evaluating staff performance. Examples of permanent products which can be used to evaluate elements of staff performance include time records, client progress notes written by staff, client evaluations, or any of the various forms of documentation generated by staff in human service agencies. In these cases, the quality of the documentation is evaluated by the supervisor once staff have completed the documentation in contrast to observing staff actually write the information. Staff work activities producing changes in the physical work environment can also be measured as outcomes. Examples of performance activities producing changes in many human service work environments include client and environmental cleanliness, availability of leisure materials, and therapeutic body positions of nonambulatory clients.

There are several distinct advantages of outcome-based or permanent product monitoring. Most notably, this type of monitoring can be performed at the supervisor's convenience because staff do not have to be present and engaging in the work when monitoring occurs. For example, to evaluate staffs' performance in maintaining a clean and orderly living room in a half way house for adults with psychiatric impairment, the supervisor could observe the cleanliness and orderliness of the living room when he happens to be present even if staff are working in another room in the home or outside the house. Because permanent product monitoring can be conducted without directly monitoring staff performance, it is less likely to cause disruptions in work routines than other monitoring systems involving direct observations of staff work activity. Also, staff are usually more comfortable with outcome-based monitoring compared to monitoring procedures involving a direct observation of their ongoing job performance.

Reducing Staffs' Negative Reactions to Monitoring

As noted earlier in this chapter, staff members' initial reactions to having their performance systematically monitored is usually negative. Staff reactions can range from mild nervousness to open hostility. Staffs' negative view of monitoring is not surprising when considering how performance monitoring is conducted in many human service agencies. Formal monitoring by supervisors typically occurs infrequently, and usually only when a supervisor suspects staff are doing something wrong. Subsequently, the monitoring is predictably followed by staff reprimands. The purpose of monitoring in these situations is to "catch staff being bad" and to punish them. As a result, monitoring becomes synonymous with punishment; monitoring signals staff to get ready for bad things to happen.

In contrast to the typical monitoring process just noted, in an OBM approach monitoring is a routine, positive part of supervision. If supervisors follow the recommended steps specified by an OBM approach (see Chapters 4 and 5 for more detailed discussion of positive staff training and management procedures), monitoring should be followed by positive recognition for job performance far more often than a reprimand. Therefore, over time staffs' negative reactions to having their performance monitored are decreased because monitoring becomes a signal for good things to come. In fact, if the supervisor is successful at creating a highly motivating work environment from an overall perspective, staff even begin to look forward to having their performance monitored (see Chapter 8 for elaboration).

Staff report being more comfortable with having their performance monitored when they are aware of what work activities are being monitored and how the monitoring process will occur. Actually, there is no legitimate reason why staff should not be familiar with the monitoring process if the purpose of monitoring is to obtain information for objectively evaluating staff performance. Further, if the goal is also to monitor staff performance as one step in creating a motivating work environment, supervisors should be open and honest about the fact monitoring will occur and what the monitoring process will entail.

Deliberately being secretive about monitoring procedures should not be common practice because it breeds an atmosphere of suspicion and mistrust. Being secretive about monitoring (i.e., not letting staff know their performance is being monitored) is only called for when there is very good reason to suspect staff are engaging in illegal or immoral activities in the work place, such as stealing, drug use, and client abuse or neglect. Of course when illegal or immoral activities are suspected, the purpose of monitoring is not to evaluate staff performance but to catch the guilty staff and to fire them. Otherwise, when monitoring is conducted within the context of routine supervision, supervisors should be candid and above board about how staff performance will be monitored. Taking the time to familiarize staff with monitoring systems will reduce staffs' negative reactions toward monitoring and in the long run, contribute to a more motivating work environment for staff. We have found a simple yet effective process for familiarizing staff with monitoring procedures that requires very little time on the part of supervisors. Prior to conducting any observations of staff performance, each staff person should be given a copy of the monitoring form. As staff review the form, the exact procedures for observing and recording performance should be explained by the supervisor. Staff should then watch as the supervisor demonstrates the work activity, and record the supervisor's performance on the monitoring form according to the previously specified monitoring procedures. By having staff use the monitoring system to evaluate the supervisor's performance, the monitoring process tends to be "demystified" for staff and reduces staffs' discomfort with having their own performance monitored.

STAFF SHOULD KNOW THEIR PERFORMANCE IS BEING MONITORED AND KNOW WHY THE MONITORING IS OCCURRING

Another way supervisors can decrease staff discomfort with monitoring is to discuss results of the monitoring session with staff as soon as possible after monitoring is completed. Immediate feedback about the monitoring can eliminate anxiety staff experience while waiting to hear from the supervisor concerning the observation. When the situation does not permit a detailed discussion of the staff member's performance immediately following an observation, the supervisor should still strive to make either a positive statement (e.g., "Things look good; I'll get back to you on this just before shift change this afternoon.") or at least an empathetic statement (e.g., "I know it is difficult to work with someone looking over your shoulder; we'll go over this after the children leave.") immediately following the observation. Chapter 5 discusses in- depth guidelines for making supervisory feedback acceptable to staff.

Perhaps the most critical guideline for fostering a positive attitude among staff regarding performance monitoring is one that should be obvious — Be nice!Being nice means using a pleasant tone of voice, smiling, greeting staff prior to conducting an observation and thanking them when the observation is complete. Being nice also means making an effort to be unobtrusive and nondisruptive to the staffs' ongoing work when conducting observations. When initiating a monitoring session, supervisors should not only greet the staff person, but also briefly state the reason for the visit and then conduct the monitoring session as inconspicuously as possible.

Being nice further entails refraining from conducting routine observations during atypical or emergency situations in the work place. For example, if a client becomes extremely disruptive or upset during a staff monitoring session, monitoring should be immediately discontinued. The supervisor should abandon the monitoring and assist the staff member as dictated by the situation, or at least leave the situation if the supervisor does not have the time to assist due to competing responsibilities. If monitoring were to continue throughout a situation like the one just described, the result would likely be an unfair evaluation of staffs' performance as well as extremely distressed staff persons.

SUMMARY OF GUIDELINES FOR ENHANCING STAFF ACCEPTANCE OF PERFORMANCE MONITORING

1. Inform staff monitoring will occur
2. Routinely monitor staff performance, not just in response to problems
3. Familiarize staff with monitoring procedures
4. Provide immediate feedback following monitoring
5. When monitoring, be nice: pleasant, unobtrusive, discontinue monitoring during atypical situations

Chapter 4

ENHANCING WORK PERFORMANCE THROUGH STAFF TRAINING

As discussed in preceding chapters, direct service staff make up the largest segment of the work force in most human service agencies. Because of the large number of direct service personnel, the proficiency with which these staff perform their jobs is a major determinant of the quality of an agency's services. The pervasive influence of direct service staff exists even though these individuals begin their human service jobs with essentially no formal preparation or job training. Consequently, a substantial amount of time and resources must be directed toward training work skills to direct service personnel if human service agencies are to provide quality services for clients. This chapter describes OBM procedures specifically for training a wide variety of important work skills to direct service staff in the human services.

The Role of Staff Training in Human Services

Before discussing strategies for training direct service staff, it is important to clarify the role of staff training within the overall context of supervision. Specifically, although the nature and size of the direct service work force necessitates a significant amount of training, staff training is only one component of effective supervision. We emphasize this characteristic of staff training because in many human service agencies, management personnel overly rely on training programs to resolve serious problems with staff performance. Many if not most significant performance problems involve staff having the skills to perform their work, but not using those skills appropriately to fulfill daily responsibilities. If staff have the necessary work skills but are not performing satisfactorily on the day-to-day job, implementing a staff training program will not resolve the performance problems.

In the type of situation just noted, typically staff have already been trained in the necessary work skills to perform their jobs but effective supervisory procedures have not been employed following training to ensure staff adequately use their skills. Chapter 5 provides an in-depth discussion of supervisory strategies for ensuring satisfactory performance following training. The point of concern here is that providing staff with training will set the occasion for staff to perform proficiently, but training alone usually will not result in proficient job performance on a routine basis. In short, staff training is often necessary for ensuring competent job performance, but rarely sufficient. Hence, we describe procedures for successfully training staff to perform their direct service jobs with the qualification that such training is only an initial step — albeit an important step — for ensuring satisfactory job performance.

STAFF TRAINING IS OFTEN NECESSARY BUT RARELY SUFFICIENT FOR ENSURING PROFICIENT STAFF PERFORMANCE ON THE DAY-TO-DAY JOB

Characteristics of Successful Staff Training Programs

Providing Effective Staff Training

To be successful, a staff training program must first meet one rather obvious, bottom line criterion: the program must be effective. Despite the many hours management personnel frequently invest in developing and implementing staff training programs, surprisingly few managers carefully evaluate if training is truly effective. Managers simply assume training is having the desired impact, and are satisfied to know staff have participated in a respective training program. As such, no evidence is obtained to support the assumption that the training is indeed effective. Our experience as well as a considerable amount of research suggest such an assumption is often erroneous. The vast majority of staff training programs in human service agencies are quite ineffective, resulting in no improvement in agency services.

In order to ensure agency services are truly enhanced when staff training is provided, evidence must be obtained to demonstrate the effectiveness of the training. Evidence of effectiveness should be obtained by examining two desired outcomes of staff training programs. The first outcome is staff skill acquisition — staff should acquire the job skills addressed in the training program. The second outcome is enhanced client welfare — clients should benefit in some observable way when staff apply the skills they have acquired in a training program. For example, to determine if a training program on procedures for decreasing incontinence among elderly nursing home residents is effective, a nursing home supervisor should first consider whether staff can demonstrate the (trained) skills to perform the procedures when they return to the work site. Next, if staff do demonstrate the desired skills, the supervisor should evaluate if routine use of those skills by the staff results in reduced toileting accidents among the nursing home residents. In brief, without evidence staff acquire new work skills and clients benefit from staffs' use of their skills on the job, it cannot be assumed a staff training program has been effective.

Providing Efficient Staff Training

A second characteristic related to the success of staff training programs is how efficiently training can be conducted. Efficiency of staff training is a concern in human service agencies for three reasons. First, in most agencies the time available for training new staff is limited. Direct service staff are usually needed to work directly with clients from the moment they are hired due to lean staffing patterns. Second, monetary costs necessary for training must be contained because staff training needs often exceed staff training budgets. Generally, the more efficiently staff can be trained, the lower the training cost for an agency. Third, turnover rates among direct service staff are quite high in many human service agencies. High staff turnover means the same staff training programs must be repeated as new staff continuously enter the agency. For each of these reasons, time-consuming training programs are impractical. Supervisors and other staff training personnel should strive to develop programs requiring the least amount of time to effectively train necessary skills to staff.

Providing Acceptable Staff Training

A third characteristic of successful staff training programs pertains to how acceptable training is to the staff who participate in the training. Training programs must be acceptable to staff if the programs are to be viable over the long term. If staff members find training unacceptable, they are likely to be reluctant and/or react negatively when asked or required to participate in training. In turn, the reluctance and negativism among staff make the job of the staff trainer most unpleasant. Trainers lose their motivation to conduct training with staff because the trainers essentially dread their staffs' negative reactions to having to participate in the training program. The lack of motivation to conduct training jeopardizes continued use of what may otherwise be an effective staff training program.

Due to the importance of staff acceptance of training programs, how much staff like or dislike various training procedures should be a consideration in deciding which particular procedures to use in a training program. Staff acceptance of a training program, or procedural components within a program, can be evaluated in several ways. One way is to simply ask staff which parts of a given training program they liked or disliked after they have experienced each of the training procedures. Staffs' responses to such a question can be used to refine training procedures to employ in the future with those staff as well as with other staff. Another way to evaluate staff acceptance is to ask staff to choose which methods they would prefer for future training. Subsequently, the training procedures staff choose can be incorporated into future training programs (assuming of course, the choice of procedures still includes effective training procedures). To illustrate, if staff report they dislike being videotaped as a part of a training program — which we have found to be frequently the case when using videotape — and the training can be conducted effectively without videotaping, then the videotaping should be eliminated from the overall program.

Making staff training programs as acceptable as possible has a highly important though often overlooked effect on staff motivation. As just indicated, acceptable staff training programs are more likely to be continued in an agency than unacceptable programs. Continuing programs that train important work skills is a necessary component for ensuring staff perform their work competently. Additionally, by using programs staff like, staffs' work environment is made more enjoyable relative to using programs staff dislike. Hence, relying on staff training programs that are acceptable to staff significantly enhances the work enjoyment aspect of staff motivation.

TO BE SUCCESSFUL, STAFF TRAINING PROGRAMS MUST BE EFFECTIVE, EFFICIENT AND ACCEPTABLE

Developing Successful Staff Training Programs

The most common format for training staff in human service agencies involves a group of trainees gathering in a classroom to listen as an instructor discusses a training topic. Often, the classroom presentation is accompanied by handouts of written material. This type of lecture and discussion format represents a verbal instruction model of staff training. In recent years more high-tech methods have also been used in classroom situations to present information to trainees, and particularly through the use of videotape- and computer- assisted instruction. Though the equipment involved may be more sophisticated, the latter approaches still rely essentially on a verbal instruction model for training staff.

A verbal instruction training model is best suited for training verbal skills to staff. Verbal skills involve using new terminology or conveying factual information when conversing about a topic. Watching a videotape about mental illness, for example, can convey factual information to staff in psychiatric hospitals about the characteristics of mental illness. Similarly, reading a booklet may inform preschool staff how to use correct terminology in describing the developmental stages of early childhood.

Although improving staffs' verbal skills as just exemplified is sometimes important, a more pressing need in human service agencies involves training staff how to actually carry out job duties. Specifically, the most important goal of staff training is to improve what staff do in the work place. When the focus of training is on what staff do in contrast to how staff converse, the goal is to train performance skills to staff. Staff performance skills are more likely to impact client welfare than verbal skills because clients derive little benefit from a staff member's verbal knowledge unless the knowledge is translated into action or service. For instance, clients in a congregate living facility will not necessarily be protected very well from infectious diseases contacted through body fluids if staff are trained only to verbally describe safe handling of bodily fluids. In contrast, if staff are trained how to actually handle the fluids safely during the routine job, then clients are much more likely to be protected from infections contracted through body fluids.

When the goal of staff training is to improve performance skills, traditional staff training formats relying on verbal instruction are ineffective. Simply put, talking about how to do a task and actually doing the task are different skills and require different training strategies. The following section describes an approach to staff training specifically designed for training staff how to perform designated work duties.

VERBAL INSTRUCTION APPROACHES TO STAFF TRAINING RARELY RESULT IN STAFF ACTUALLY LEARNING HOW TO PERFORM JOB DUTIES

A Prototypical Program for Training Staff Performance Skills

Applied research in OBM has resulted in a well developed technology for training performance skills to direct service staff. The technology basically consists of the seven-step process provided in the following table. The procedures presented in the table have been used to successfully train direct service staff in a wide variety of performance skills, including interacting positively with clients who have profound multiple disabilities, providing functional educational tasks to students with severe disabilities, assembling adaptive switch mechanisms for people with physical disabilities, safely intervening with clients who become aggressive, writing performance goals and objectives for students, and using sign language with people who are non-vocal. Additional work skills trained to human service staff using the process presented below are represented in the Selected Readings section of this text.

STEPS OF A PROTOTYPICAL STAFF TRAINING PROGRAM

1. Specify work skills to be taught
2. Provide staff with a checklist description of the work skills specified in Step 1
3. Verbally describe the work skills on the checklist to staff along with the rationale for the importance of the skills
4. Physically demonstrate the work skills for staff
5. Observe staff practice the targeted work skills
6. Provide corrective and/or approving feedback to staff based on their demonstration of the targeted skills
7. Continue Steps 4, 5 and 6 until staff are observed to per-form the targeted work skills correctly

To illustrate implementation of the steps of a prototypical training program, the process for training direct service staff to provide snack and mealtime choices to nonvocal individuals with profound mental retardation will be described. Providing choices to clients is an important function of essentially every human service agency. When staff present choice opportunities in a manner facilitating the expression of a preference by agency clients, clients can readily access enjoyable items and events. By increasing client access to enjoyable items and events, human service staff can significantly enhance client quality of life on a day-to-day basis.

The first two steps for training a performance skill to staff are basically the same steps for pinpointing staff performance described in Chapter 3: specifying the skill as measurable work behaviors and listing the behaviors in written format. To specify what staff should do when offering a snack choice to a nonvocal client (Step 1), the following written description could be given to staff (Step 2).

PROCEDURES FOR PRESENTING A CHOICE OF SNACK ITEMS TO A PERSON WITH PROFOUND MENTAL RETARDATION WHO IS NONVOCAL

1. Show the client two food items
2. Prompt the client to choose one of the items by saying "Which would you like?"
3. Wait at least 10 seconds for the client to respond by touching, pointing or gesturing toward one of the items
4. If the client does not respond within 10 seconds, give the client a taste of each food item and repeat steps 1 and 2
5. If the client selects one of the items, provide the selected item and remove the other item
6. If the client does not select either item after sampling both items, give the client one of the items

After the staff have read the written summary of how to provide a food choice, the trainer should describe each aspect of the process for providing food choices (Step 3). Verbally describing what staff should do is included with the written description because some staff may read poorly and are too embarrassed to ask questions that could reveal their poor reading skills. Included with the verbal description of what to do should be a rationale regarding why the staff are being trained to perform the skill.

A common mistake when conducting staff training is that staff are not provided a reasonable explanation regarding why they have to participate in the training. Being expected to learn new work skills without an explanation as to why the skills need to be acquired leads to staff discontent with the training process. In contrast, presenting a rationale for the importance of the skills being trained can greatly enhance staffs' acceptance of the training program. Staff are more willing to perform a work task if they have a good understanding of why the task is important.

Once staff have read and heard a description of the task as well as a rationale for the skill's importance, the trainer should demonstrate the skill as staff observe (Step 4). In the case of food choices, the trainer should demonstrate all the procedures for providing food choices listed in the written description. Next, each trainee should practice providing food choices while the trainer systematically observes each trainee's performance (Step 5). Systematic performance observations will usually require the trainer to develop a checklist or other observation form to assist the trainer in documenting staffs' correct or incorrect performance of each step of the skill. The observation form should list each behavioral step for completing the skill based on the written description previously given to staff. As the trainer observes staff perform the skill, each step included on the checklist should be scored as correctly or incorrectly performed. An example of a checklist for observing staff provision of food choices is presented below.

CHECKLIST FOR OBSERVING STAFF PRESENTATION OF FOOD CHOICES TO A CLIENT WITH PROFOUND MENTAL RETARDATION

Staff name: _Mike Robinson_ Date: _4/25/95_   Time: _12:15_

Skill Components   Correct implentation?

	Yes	No	N/A*
Shows client two food items.	✓		
Prompts client to choose one of the items by saying "Which would you like?"	✓		
Waits at least 10 seconds for client to respond by touching, pointing or gesturing toward one of the items.		✓	
If client does not respond within 10 seconds, gives client a taste of each item and presents the items again.	✓		
If client selects one of the items, provides selected item and removes the other item.	✓		
If client does not select either item after sampling both items, gives client one item.			✓

*N/A = Not Applicable

Observation Summary

Percentage correct performance (number of steps performed correctly divided by the number of total steps performed multiplied by 100) = _80%_

In addition to observing staff performance as just described, it is helpful if the trainer specifies the level of correct performance necessary for a staff member to master the targeted skill. Mastery criteria may require staff to demonstrate a specified level of correct performance over several observations before training is considered complete. For example, to master the skill of presenting food choices to nonvocal clients, a staff member typically must score a "yes" on all applicable components of the checklist during at least two observed choice-presentation sessions.

After each observation for a respective trainee, the trainer should review the observation form and provide diagnostic feedback to the trainee (Step 6). In order to provide diagnostic feedback effectively, two procedural components must be completed by the trainer. First, the trainer must identify the skills (or steps comprising the skill) the trainee performed correctly and provide specific praise for the correct performance. Second, the trainer must identify any steps the trainee performed incorrectly, and then describe how the steps should have been performed.

The process of a trainer providing diagnostic feedback after staff practice a skill represents the most critical element of an effective staff training program. Despite the importance of staff practice followed by trainer feedback, however, many supervisors and other staff training personnel are not skilled in providing diagnostic feedback as part of staff training programs. The lack of feedback skills relates to the problem noted in Chapter 3 of agency personnel not receiving appropriate training in how to supervise — or in this case, how to train staff — once they become supervisors. Supervisory skill in providing feedback to staff is particularly important because how feedback is provided directly affects how successful the feedback is in improving staff performance. Relatedly, how feedback is provided impacts how acceptable the feedback is to staff. To assist supervisors in providing feedback effectively, we have found it helpful to use a 7-component protocol for presenting the feedback. The feedback protocol is provided below.

PROTOCOL FOR PROVIDING DIAGNOSTIC FEEDBACK TO STAFF AS PART OF TRAINING PROGRAMS

1. Begin feedback session with positive or empathetic statement
2. Provide positive comments regarding aspects of the skill performed correctly
3. Identify skill aspects performed incorrectly
4. Identify how skill aspects identified in #3 should have been performed
5. Solicit questions or concerns from the staff trainee
6. Reference what will happen next regarding training
7. End the session with a positive statement about the trainee's performance

As indicated by the protocol just summarized, the trainer should begin the feedback presentation by setting a positive tone for the feedback session (Component 1 of the feedback protocol). To set a positive tone, the trainer should offer a general approving or empathetic comment relating to the training observation, such as "I know it feels a little awkward to offer food choices in this way but you really are doing well." Staff are likely to be feeling anxious about being observed by the trainer, and beginning the feedback session on an empathetic or positive note helps to reduce staffs' anxiety. When staff feel anxious about their performance, they not only experience an unpleasant feeling or sensation (i.e., worrying — see Chapter 6), they usually do not listen very attentively to the feedback.

Following the trainer's empathetic or positive statement, the trainer should provide specific diagnostic feedback by first pinpointing and then praising those skills performed correctly by the staff member (Component 2). For example, when providing diagnostic feedback regarding a food choice presentation the trainer might say, "You showed Mike both food items and asked him which he wanted. That was exactly the way to begin." Next, the trainer should describe any steps of the skill the trainee performed incorrectly (Component 3) and then explain what the staff person should have done to perform the steps correctly (Component 4). In the latter case, a corrective statement might be "You only waited a couple of seconds for Mike to indicate what he wanted. It is important to wait at least 10 seconds to give Mike adequate time to respond to your food choice presentation." Subsequently, to make certain the trainee understands the feedback, the trainer should ask the trainee if she has any questions regarding the feedback just provided (Component 5).

After the trainer's response to any questions the staff trainee may have, the trainer should reference what should happen next based on the outcome of the observation (Component 6). To illustrate, if the trainee performed poorly, the trainer might indicate the need to observe the trainee again within a few days and instruct the trainee to practice the skill using the suggestions for improvement. In contrast, if the trainee has met the mastery criterion for providing food choices, the trainer could indicate no additional training observations are necessary. By referencing what should happen next, the trainer communicates a commitment to continuing the observations and feedback until the staff member reaches the training criterion. Such information prevents the staff person from thinking training is completed and that he no longer needs to be concerned about the skills addressed in the training program.

The final component of feedback should be a positive or encouraging statement (Component 7). For instance, a trainer might end the feedback with a statement such as "Thanks for allowing me to observe. Overall, you are doing a nice job of providing choice during the meal." By ending a feedback session on an upbeat or encouraging note, staff are likely to view the feedback in a positive light, even if corrective feedback was given earlier in the session.

Classroom-Based Versus On-The-Job Training

In planning for staff training, careful consideration should be given to where the training is conducted. Options regarding where to train staff basically involve conducting the training in a classroom-type setting away from the routine work environment versus conducting on-the-job training in the regular work setting while staff engage in their usual work routines. There are advantages and disadvantages of conducting training in each of these settings.

Conducting training in a classroom setting typically has the advantage of time efficiency relative to conducting training in staffs' regular work place. In particular, classroom-based training allows a group of staff to be trained at once whereas on-the-job training usually can be conducted with only one staff person at a time. In a classroom setting, trainees are also less likely to be distracted by client needs, and trainees can concentrate more readily on learning the skill being trained. However, a major disadvantage of classroom-based training relates to the effectiveness with which performance skills are trained. Performance skills trained in a classroom setting often do not carryover to the routine work environment. Staff may demonstrate proficiency in performing a skill in the classroom, but because the classroom setting is different from the regular work setting staff cannot perform the skill in the latter environment. In contrast, training performance skills within staffs' regular work site eliminates any concern regarding carryover of trained skills. Due to the difficulty in extending performance skills trained in the classroom to staffs' usual work site, training of performance skills should not be conducted exclusively in a classroom setting.

A reasonable compromise between the time efficiency of classroom-based training and the effectiveness of on-the-job training is to initially conduct a portion of the training in a classroom setting and then complete the training in staffs' routine work site. For example, descriptions of the skills to be trained and the rationale for the skills can be provided to a group of trainees in a classroom. The classroom training can also involve opportunities for the trainer to demonstrate the performance skills and for trainees to practice the skills using role play techniques.

Role playing involves creating simulated conditions in the classroom that are as similar as possible to the regular work environment. The more similar the training environment is to the work environment in which the skills are to be routinely performed, the more likely skills learned in the classroom will carry over to the routine work setting. Role playing allows trainees to practice new skills and receive diagnostic feedback from the trainer. To illustrate, when training staff to conduct teaching sessions with clients who have severe disabilities, trainees could practice client-teaching skills in a classroom setting by teaching another staff member who plays the role of a client. The practice sessions would be observed by the staff trainer who provides diagnostic feedback to the staff. The entire process should be continued until each staff trainee demonstrates proficient client teaching in the simulated situation.

Once staff have demonstrated competence in performing new work skills in the classroom-based, role-playing situation, on-the-job observation of staffs' target skills in the regular work place should occur. If the on-the-job observations indicate staff do not perform the skills proficiently, continued training of the target skills must be conducted in the work site. The work site training should involve staff practice of the work skills with trainer feedback similar to the process followed with the role playing in the classroom. Typically though, after trainees have demonstrated proficiency in performing a skill in the classroom, only a few observations with feedback are likely to be needed for trainees to meet specified mastery criteria on the job. The important point is a skill cannot be considered mastered by a staff member until the trainer observes the staff member perform the target work skill correctly on the job.

STAFF TRAINING SHOULD NEVER BE CONSIDERED COMPLETE UNTIL THE TRAINER OBSERVES EACH STAFF TRAINEE CORRECTLY PERFORM THE TARGETED WORK SKILLS IN THE REGULAR WORK ENVIRONMENT

Making On-The-Job Observations Acceptable to Staff

As previously discussed in this chapter as well as in Chapter 3, being observed by a supervisor or training instructor is a situation most staff dislike. Hence, because performance observations and staff acceptance of the observations are both essential ingredients of successful staff training programs, supervisors must take specific actions to make training observations as likable as possible. Through a combination of research and experience, we have found several helpful strategies supervisors can use to increase staff acceptance of having their work performance observed.

One strategy for enhancing staff acceptance of performance observations is to ensure staff are familiar with the process used to monitor their performance. Familiarizing staff with the monitoring process should occur before any training observations are initiated. The reader is referred to the discussion in Chapter 3 regarding a quick method for familiarizing staff with monitoring procedures as a means of increasing the acceptability of performance monitoring.

In addition to familiarizing staff with the monitoring process prior to observing their performance, staff should be informed in advance exactly when they will be observed performing the skills addressed in the training program. If staff know when observations will occur, they can be prepared to demonstrate the skills to the best of their ability. Staff will feel more comfortable during the initial observations of their performance if they are prepared for the observations. In contrast, if staff are observed without forewarning and feel unprepared, their anxiety level is likely to be at an uncomfortable level.

How feedback is provided to staff after observations of their performance can also affect staff acceptance of the observations. In particular, how quickly feedback is provided following the observations affects how much staff like or dislike the observations. The less time elapsing between a performance observation and the supervisor's feedback, the less time staff spend wondering and worrying about the outcome of the observation. Consequently, if feedback is provided immediately after observations, the amount of worry and anxiety staff experience is minimized. The format for providing feedback can likewise impact staffs' acceptance of performance observations. Specifically, most staff prefer to receive spoken feedback accompanied by a written summary of the feedback in contrast to spoken feedback alone.

STAFF ACCEPTANCE OF OBSERVATIONS OF THEIR PERFORMANCE CAN BE INCREASED BY

- Familiarizing staff with observation procedures
- Informing staff when training observations will occur
- Providing feedback immediately following an observation
- Providing a brief written summary of feedback in addition to spoken feedback

Involving the Supervisor in Staff Training

One element influencing the overall success of any staff training endeavor is the degree of involvement of the staff supervisor in the training process. Supervisors should be directly involved in staff training and where possible, actually conduct the training themselves. Supervisors generally are more aware of their staffs' training needs than other individuals who may be employed as training instructors (e.g., staff development personnel, consultants hired from outside the agency) and consequently, can make the training more relevant to staffs' routine job expectations. Often, skills thought to be important by staff trainers — who are less familiar with the daily job of direct service staff than staff supervisors — are not viewed as important skills by direct service personnel. Supervisors also make important decisions affecting staffs' quality of work life, such as pay raises, work schedules and promotions. Therefore, staff are more motivated to learn skills trained by their supervisor relative to skills trained by instructors who do not control such decisions. From the standpoint of supervisors, conducting staff training themselves helps ensure the supervisors are competent in the skills expected of their staff. As discussed in Chapter 8, a supervisor's job in regard to motivating staff is facilitated immeasurably if the supervisor is skilled at performing the same jobs staff are expected to perform.

Despite the noted advantages associated with supervisors conducting staff training, supervisors will not always be in the best position to function as a staff trainer. Supervisors may not have enough time to conduct all the training required by their staff while adequately performing the myriad of other duties required by supervisory jobs. Additionally, some supervisors are not sufficiently skilled in all aspects of staff training to serve as effective staff trainers. In such situations, staff training personnel other than the staff supervisor can successfully train staff if they work in close conjunction with the supervisor. A reasonable merging of training efforts in the latter case is for staff training personnel to conduct classroom-based components of training and supervisors to conduct on-the-job observation and feedback components. The important point is staff training programs are much more likely to be successful when staff supervisors are integrally and visibly involved in the staff training process.

Chapter 5

ENHANCING AND MAINTAINING STAFF PERFORMANCE THROUGH ON-THE-JOB FEEDBACK

In preceding chapters we have discussed three types of supervisory actions for enhancing diligent and proficient staff performance. To summarize briefly, a supervisor begins the process of ensuring desired staff performance by first pinpointing or defining performance expectations (Chapter 3). Next, identified performance duties are monitored to determine if actual performance is commensurate with expected performance (Chapter 3). If the monitoring reveals staff are not performing a particular job duty adequately, staff training may then be required to help staff develop the skills for performing the duty more proficiently (Chapter 4).

Although performance pinpointing, monitoring and training are frequently necessary for ensuring adequate work performance, as indicated in Chapter 4 with staff training, these supervisory practices are rarely sufficient for ensuring staff adequately fulfill their work responsibilities on a day-to-day basis. Rather, what usually determines the adequacy of work performance day in and day out is the consequence resulting from the performance. Supervisors can have a powerful effect on the quality of staffs' on-the-job performance by arranging the kinds of consequences that follow both desirable and undesirable work performance. The following grid provides a simple framework for conceptualizing how consequences can be used to maximize desirable work performance and minimize undesirable performance.

Framework for Applying
PerformanceConsequences

Supervisor's Job	Staff Person's Performance	
	Desirable	Undesirable
Provide a positive consequence	(1) Do	(2) Don't
Provide a negative consequence	(3) Don't	(4) Sometimes

The upper left-hand corner of the grid (1) represents the optimal use of performance consequences: positive consequences should follow desirable staff performance. When a staff member works a double shift to cover for an ill employee, for example, the supervisor may arrange for the staff member to have three consecutive days off the next week. Assuming having consecutive days off is desirable for the staff person, the supervisor is ensuring a positive consequence results from the staff person's extra work efforts. By arranging a positive consequence to follow desirable work performance in this manner, the supervisor is reinforcing, or strengthening, that particular performance. In turn, by reinforcing the staff member's work performance, the supervisor is increasing the likelihood the staff person will volunteer to work in the future during staff shortages.

BY PROVIDING A POSITIVE CONSEQUENCE FOR DESIRABLE WORK PERFORMANCE, A SUPERVISOR INCREASES THE LIKELIHOOD STAFF WILL PERFORM THEIR WORK DUTIES IN A DESIRABLE MANNER IN THE FUTURE

The use of positive consequences to reinforce desirable staff performance is a potent supervisory tool for ensuring staff routinely work diligently and proficiently. The ability and willingness to frequently reinforce desirable work performance represents a supervisor's most important contribution for establishing and maintaining a quality human service agency. Using consequences in this manner has such a significant impact because positively reinforcing desirable performance enhances not only work effort and proficiency, but also staff work enjoyment. As such, frequent positive reinforcement forms the core of successful staff motivation.

This chapter focuses on how a supervisor can use positive consequences to ensure diligent and competent work performance among staff. Subsequent chapters emphasize how supervisors can use positive consequences and related procedures to enhance staff enjoyment in the work place. However, it should also be noted that depending on how they are used (see preceding consequence grid), consequences can have effects on staff performance other than reinforcing desirable work habits and increasing work enjoyment. Effects of these other uses of performance consequences — which represent in essence, supervisory mistakes — can be quite detrimental from a staff motivational perspective. Hence, before discussing the optimal use of performance consequences, common supervisory mistakes involving consequence presentation warrant mention.

ROUTINE USE OF POSITIVE REINFORCEMENT IS THE CORE OF SUCCESSFUL STAFF MOTIVATION

In contrast to the highly advantageous strategy of using positive consequences to reinforce desirable work performance, the upper right-hand section of the consequence grid (2) reflects a use of positive consequences supervisors should strive to avoid. Specifically, positive consequences should not be provided following undesirable staff performance. The latter practice has the effect of supervisors reinforcing undesirable work habits.

Supervisors typically do not reinforce undesirable performance by intentionally providing a positive consequence for the performance. However, unintentional provision of positive consequences following undesirable performance occurs on a regular basis in many human service agencies. A common example is when a supervisor waits for one individual who is late before beginning an important meeting. In this case, a positive consequence (the late staff member obtains the important information presented at the meeting) follows undesirable performance (tardiness). Perhaps the most extreme misuse of positive consequences for undesirable performance though, is when a staff member who performs incompetently is promoted to a higher ranking job. How and why these and other types of consequence mistakes occur is discussed in subsequent chapters. The point here is supervisors should strive to ensure positive consequences are provided only for desirable work performance among staff.

The lower left-hand corner of the consequence grid (3) also represents a supervisory mistake: providing a negative consequence following desirable performance. In contrast to positive consequences, negative consequences decrease the likelihood the performance resulting in the consequence will occur again. An illustration of this type of consequence mistake is when tedious and effortful work duties are assigned to the hardest working staff. Here, the negative consequence of being assigned extra, unpleasant work tasks follows desirable work performance. Supervisors typically fall into this consequence-mistake trap when they want certain duties to be performed well, and therefore assign the duties to staff whom the supervisors know always work diligently and competently. As a result of this practice, staff learn that routinely displaying effortful and proficient work is likely to result in more hard (and unpleasant) work being assigned to them. Another example of a negative consequence following desirable performance is when one staff member works out a resolution to a challenging agency problem yet another staff person receives recognition for the accomplishment. In this situation, the erroneous recognition for the latter staff person's lack of performance represents a negative consequence for the former person's effective performance. In both of the examples just noted, the supervisor inadvertently decreases the likelihood that desirable performance will occur in the future.

As indicated by the lower right-hand section of the grid (4), providing negative consequences for undesirable performance can sometimes be an effective method of improving staff performance. Negative consequences following undesirable work performance will decrease the likelihood of the same undesirable performance in the future. When a staff member is criticized for errors made during an emergency fire drill, for example, the staff member is usually less likely to make the same errors in the future. However, although negative consequences may decrease an undesirable aspect of staff performance in some cases, the decrease almost always comes at the expense of staff motivation. Few staff can do their best work in an environment where supervision is frequently meted out in the form of criticism and reprimands. Frequent provision of negative consequences produces resentful and unmotivated staff members.

Reliance on the use of negative consequences as an approach to supervision has detrimental effects on both the work enjoyment and work effort aspects of motivation. From the enjoyment perspective, the detrimental effects of negative consequences are quite straightforward: receiving frequent criticism, reprimands, complaints, etc., from a supervisor is not enjoyable for staff. In short, the more frequently a supervisor provides negative consequences for staff performance, the less enjoyment staff experience in the work place.

The detrimental effects of frequent use of negative consequences on the work effort aspect of motivation are more complex than the effects on work enjoyment. When supervisors rely on a negative approach to supervision, they do two things routinely. First, the supervisors frequently complain about, or chastise, staff for not performing up to expectations. Second, the supervisors heavily criticize or reprimand staff when staff make obvious mistakes in the work place. The primary effect of these supervisory practices is staff become motivated to perform their duties in order to avoid the supervisor's complaints, criticism and reprimands. In essence, staff focus their work attention and efforts on not letting the supervisor catch them doing anything wrong.

The primary problem with using negative consequences to motivate staff as just described is the process works only when the threat of the supervisor's negative actions are present. Whenever the supervisor is not around staffs' immediate work site, staff are not worried about "being caught" by the supervisor and hence, decrease their motivation to work. For example, if a supervisor in a group home for children with disabilities routinely reprimands staff when she catches them not following the activity schedule, staff will tend to follow the schedule only when the supervisor is in the group home. When the supervisor is not in the home, staff are not worried about being criticized for not following the schedule and consequently, staff do not worry about schedule compliance.

SUPERVISORY RELIANCE ON NEGATIVE CONSEQUENCES TO MANAGE STAFF PERFORMANCE ULTIMATELY IMPEDES BOTH THE WORK EFFORT AND WORK ENJOYMENT ASPECTS OF STAFF MOTIVATION

Managing through the use of negative consequences results in an unproductive game in which supervisors strive to catch staff performing poorly and staff strive to concoct ways to avoid being caught. In the long run, providing positive consequences for desirable staff performance is a much more productive supervisory strategy. As described in subsequent chapters, the types of positive consequences for supervisors to use in this manner can take many forms depending on staff preferences. Positive consequences can include an array of tangible items and events such as incentive pay, special privileges, prizes or awards. The Selected Readings section of this text, as well as Chapters 6 and 8, refer to numerous examples of how tangible consequences can improve desirable staff performance.

Although tangible consequences can be effective as just described, often such consequences are too expensive and impractical to provide on a routine basis. Due to the difficulty in providing tangible consequences routinely, we do not focus on these types of positive consequences for ensuring diligent and competent work performance on a day-to-day basis. To effectively ensure staff perform their daily duties in a desirable manner, positive consequences must be provided frequently and regularly. In many cases, positive consequences must be provided at least daily.

The remaining sections of this chapter focus on one type of consequence procedure that can be provided routinely: performance feedback. Feedback is the most readily available consequence for ensuring desirable staff performance day in and day out. When presented appropriately by supervisors, positive performance feedback also increases staff enjoyment with their work life.

Performance Feedback

Performance feedback consists of descriptive information provided directly to a staff member about the quality or quantity of the staff person's past work performance. In practice, performance feedback is most effective when the descriptive comments also include an expression of the supervisor's evaluative opinion of the performance. Telling a staff member who has an absenteeism problem, for example, "You have used 12 hours of unscheduled leave time in the past three months" illustrates the descriptive information component of feedback. An evaluative component could be included by adding comments such as "This is a big improvement compared to the 32 hours used during the same time period last year. That's great!". The latter comments inform the staff member what the supervisor thinks of her performance. When descriptive and evaluative information are included in feedback, the staff member learns how to perform in the future to gain the supervisor's approval.

Because of the importance of both descriptive and evaluative components of performance feedback, throughout this text "feedback" refers to the provision of both types of information to a staff member about past performance.

PERFORMANCE FEEDBACK SHOULD INCLUDE AN EXPLICIT REFERENCE TO THE WORK PERFORMANCE OF CONCERN PLUS AN EVALUATIVE SUMMARY OF THE STAFF PERSON'S WORK

Successful supervisors quickly realize feedback is a valuable management tool. Such supervisors spend a significant portion of the workday observing staff work performance and providing staff with feedback regarding the quality and quantity of their work. A supervisor's sincere opinion of a staff member's work, as expressed through feedback, usually matters a great deal to staff. After all, as stressed throughout this text, the actions of a supervisor heavily influence the quality of a staff member's work life. Supervisors generally assign work duties, approve leave time, and recommend pay raises, promotions or employment termination. Because a supervisor's opinion of their work is important to staff, positive feedback from the supervisor functions as a positively reinforcing consequence. Hence, by routinely providing feedback, supervisors can easily reinforce proficient performance of specific work duties — which enhances staffs' likelihood of continuing to perform the duties proficiently every day.

Although feedback is usually thought of in terms of a spoken interaction with a staff member, information about how a supervisor views performance can be conveyed in many different ways. This chapter describes an array of performance feedback strategies proven to be effective in improving or maintaining desirable staff performance. Examples of each strategy will be presented as well as the advantages and disadvantages of each strategy. Before elaborating on specific feedback strategies though, two general guidelines relevant for providing any type of performance feedback warrant discussion.

Two Important Guidelines for Providing Performance Feedback

Accentuate the Positive. In Chapter 4 it was noted that providing negative or corrective feedback may be necessary from time to time to point out staff errors or to suggest better ways to complete a work task. Using negative feedback in this manner usually improves staff performance rather quickly (although often the improvement is only temporary — see earlier comments in this chapter). Because corrective feedback frequently results in immediate improvements in staff performance, supervisors can become tempted to respond quickly to most performance problems by providing negative feedback. As pointed out previously however, overreliance on negative feedback seriously damages the motivational quality of the work environment, and works against diligent staff performance in the long run. To guard against the detrimental effects of an overly punishing work environment brought about by frequent negative feedback, supervisors should make a habit of providing far more positive than corrective feedback. A 4:1 ratio is a generally accepted rule of thumb for balancing positive and corrective feedback. Following the 4:1 guideline, every time a staff person receives negative or corrective feedback, supervisors should arrange for the staff member to receive at least four instances of positive feedback.

When supervisors are successful in following the 4:1 guideline, three worthwhile outcomes will be achieved from a staff motivational perspective. First, staff will receive a considerable amount of positive feedback. Second, supervisors will be judicious in their use of negative feedback. Third, when negative feedback is necessary, supervisors will be able to provide the mildest forms of negative feedback and still achieve improvements in staff performance. The latter effect of focusing on positive feedback is discussed more in-depth in Chapter 8.

Be Sincere. For positive feedback to have an enhancing effect on staff performance, the feedback must be sincere. If supervisors are not genuinely interested in improving an aspect of staff performance, then providing sincere positive feedback is going to be difficult. Fortunately, most supervisors usually are sufficiently concerned about the work their staff are performing to be truly pleased when staff are doing well. Even the most dedicated supervisor though runs the risk of being insincere at times. To illustrate, a supervisor may be very interested in initially improving an aspect of poor performance but when the performance subsequently reaches the desired level of proficiency, the supervisor loses interest in that particular work area. Maintaining the desirable performance is just not as exciting or interesting for the supervisor as achieving the initial improvement in performance. In such a case, the supervisor's presentation of feedback to staff regarding the work performance is likely to become half-hearted over time.

Another circumstance setting the occasion for insincere feedback is when a supervisor is required by superiors to give feedback about a performance area the supervisor does not consider very important. This situation can occur when a senior manager's priorities for client service and related staff performance conflict with the priorities of the staffs' immediate supervisor. A supervisor in a group home for clients with serious physical disabilities, for example, may view staffs' completion of health care and medical routines as far more important than client-teaching sessions that the supervisor's boss wants staff to conduct throughout the day. In the latter case, the supervisor is likely to find herself dispensing hollow feedback to staff about client-teaching sessions because she is presenting the feedback only because she has been told to provide feedback, not because she is seriously concerned about staffs' teaching of clients.

Sincerity is difficult to fake and staff will quickly detect a supervisor's shallow interest in their performance. When feedback is provided without genuine concern or interest in a staff person's performance, the feedback will not be experienced as positive by the staff person. Consequently, the feedback is unlikely to reinforce performance. In such situations, supervisors will need to find some means of motivating staff other than feedback.

MOST FEEDBACK SHOULD BE POSITIVE AND ALL FEEDBACK SHOULD BE SINCERE

Selecting A Feedback Mechanism

Feedback can be delivered in many different ways. When determining which particular way to use at a given point in time, two factors should be considered. The first factor is which mechanism will be most effective with a respective staff person. Again, to have an enhancing effect on work performance, feedback must be reinforcing. Because staff differ in terms of what they find reinforcing, how feedback is delivered should be determined by considering individual staff preferences.

The second factor to consider when selecting a feedback mechanism is how convenient or practical a particular mechanism is for the supervisor. Focusing on practical supervisory strategies — such as those requiring minimal time to implement — greatly facilitates a supervisor's job of motivating his staff. To assist supervisors in selecting the most suitable feedback mechanism, a variety of feedback procedures are described in the following chapter sections.

Vocal Feedback. Most human service supervisors report they use vocal feedback as a management tool. Vocal feedback involves a face-to-face, spoken interaction between a supervisor and staff member. Vocal feedback may be as simple as telling a staff person in passing he did a nice job preparing a client evaluation, or as complex as an item-by-item discussion of an assessment tool a staff member developed for screening potential clients.

As previously mentioned, vocal feedback should include both descriptive and evaluative information about performance. To review briefly, descriptive information should clarify the precise part of the staff member's performance being addressed by the supervisor. For example, telling a day care staff member she had all of her students involved in an activity when observed yesterday specifies for the staff person what aspect of her performance is of concern. Evaluative information indicates whether the supervisor views the specified work as praiseworthy. Using the same example with the day care staff person, the supervisor could include both descriptive and evaluative information with a comment such as "When I came by your class yesterday I was pleased to see you had all the children involved in an activity. I know consistent involvement in activities is hard to do with this age group, yet you are really keeping involvement at a high level. Keep up the good work."

Vocal feedback as just described can make the day care staff person feel good about what she has done, and feeling good about one's performance is reinforcing. The feedback also helps ensure the staff person is aware the supervisor views involving children in activities as important. Relatedly, the staff person learns involving all of her students in activities on a routine basis will set the occasion for her to receive more commendation from her supervisor in the future.

There are several distinct advantages of vocal feedback as a means of enhancing desirable work performance. First, vocal feedback is frequently quite effective in changing or maintaining work performance. The staff management literature is replete with demonstrations of the performance enhancement function of vocal feedback. Second, vocal feedback is extremely practical. Vocal feedback requires little preparation, can be delivered immediately after an observation of staff performance, and requires minimal or no financial cost to an agency.

A third advantage of vocal feedback is somewhat less obvious than effectiveness and practicality, but no less important. Specifically, the face-to-face interaction between a staff member and supervisor during vocal feedback provides valuable information for the supervisor. Observing a staff person's reaction to vocal feedback provides useful information to the supervisor regarding whether or not vocal feedback is a pleasant experience for the staff member. Such information allows the supervisor to tailor more reinforcing feedback experiences for individual staff in the future. Additionally, when a staff member reacts positively to the supervisor's feedback, the staff person's pleasant reaction can be reinforcing to the supervisor. Consequently, the supervisor becomes more willing to provide vocal feedback in the future. The mutual exchange of feedback and reinforcement inherent in vocal feedback makes this type of feedback mechanism popular among supervisors who routinely provide performance feedback to their staff.

POSITIVE VOCAL FEEDBACK IS THE MOST READILY AVAILABLE MEANS OF REINFORCING DESIRABLE STAFF PERFORMANCE

Vocal feedback also has its disadvantages. In particular, receiving praise for performance during a face-to-face interaction may not be reinforcing for some staff. Staff may feel embarrassed about receiving compliments concerning their work and/or be unsure how to react. Such feelings usually occur among staff who have rarely received positive vocal feedback from previous supervisors. These staff have not had the opportunity to learn how to act when a supervisor expresses commendation or gratitude for their work performance. When vocal feedback results in awkwardness or discomfort among staff, the interaction is not a gratifying experience for either the supervisor or the staff, regardless of the supervisor's good intentions. In these situations, supervisors may need to use another mechanism for providing feedback to staff which does not create the discomfort associated with face-to-face interactions.

Another disadvantage of vocal feedback is a supervisor's positive comments may be interpreted as manipulative by the receiving staff person. Staff may speculate the supervisor is "buttering them up" to gain some personal advantage. In these situations, misinterpretation of the purpose of the feedback may be due to the supervisor's lack of skill in presenting vocal feedback—the supervisor may not seem very sincere in her feedback comments. In this regard, some supervisors may be very sincere but do not appear sincere, and especially supervisors who are unaccustomed to giving vocal feedback. In the latter case, expressing sincerity should improve with the supervisor's practice in giving vocal feedback. However, providing reinforcing vocal feedback may never be a strength for some supervisors; some supervisors simply do not feel comfortable saying very many positive things to their staff. When supervisors do not feel comfortable providing vocal feedback, other feedback mechanisms can be utilized that do not require a direct interaction between the supervisor and staff.

VOCAL FEEDBACK MUST BE SINCERE AND MUST APPEAR SINCERE

Written Feedback. A common alternative to the use of vocal feedback is providing feedback in written format. Written feedback may be as simple as a brief, informal note from a school principal to a teacher thanking him for allowing visitors to observe his class. Written feedback can also be much more complex, such as a completed, comprehensive checklist indicating correct and incorrect performance of each step of a client lifting procedure performed by direct service staff in a nursing home (see Chapter 3 for description of performance checklists).

Written feedback offers several advantages over vocal feedback. First, written feedback does not require a face-to-face interaction with a staff member. Hence, written feedback can be a better option than vocal feedback for supervisors who are not interpersonally skillful in providing vocal feedback, as well as for staff who feel uncomfortable receiving vocal feedback from their supervisor. Second, written feedback may be more practical in work settings in which meeting directly with staff is difficult to arrange. To illustrate, it may be more efficient for a supervisor who manages group homes across a large geographical area to prepare written comments about previously observed staff performance and forward the comments to staff in contrast to traveling to each staff member's work site to give vocal feedback.

A third advantage of written feedback is it results in a permanent record regarding staff performance. A permanent record of performance can be beneficial because it allows staff to review the feedback any time after it is received. Repeated reviews of written feedback may be particularly helpful when the feedback is highly detailed and difficult to absorb in one presentation. A written record of performance can also be advantageous in that some staff view written information as a more significant consequence than vocal feedback because it permanently documents the quality or quantity of their work.

Written feedback also has several distinct disadvantages as a feedback mechanism. First, although the elimination of the face-to-face interaction between staff and supervisor inherent in written feedback is sometimes an advantage, it can also be a serious disadvantage. With written feedback, supervisors miss an opportunity to directly observe staffs' reactions to the feedback—reactions that can be helpful to supervisors for adjusting future feedback practices. A second disadvantage of written feedback is the increased effort associated with preparing written feedback relative to vocal feedback. Preparing a written note requires more of a supervisor's time (and perhaps a secretary's time if written feedback is formally prepared) than simply speaking with a staff member. The effort required of supervisors to prepare written material can result in supervisors providing infrequent feedback, and infrequent feedback often portends an increase in staff performance problems.

One means of reducing the effort of giving written feedback is to utilize preprinted forms with standard information. The standard information can reduce the amount of writing the supervisor has to complete each time written feedback is prepared. When written feedback is brief in nature, for example, a standard form such as that presented on the following page can be prepared for giving feedback on many different types of work performance. The "Commendation Award" as illustrated can be printed and duplicated on 4" X 6" cards. Using the "Commendation Award" the supervisor simply fills in the blanks on the form by indicating what aspect of a staff person's performance was deemed praiseworthy. Completing the form usually only requires a few minutes of a supervisor's time and when completed, the supervisor can easily send the form to the staff person through the agency's mail system. If the feedback is to be private, the form can be folded in the middle with the bottom edges sealed together so the written information can be viewed only by the staff recipient who opens the form.

Example of Form for Giving Brief Written Feedback

COMMENDATION AWARD

I commend the job you are doing for our agency because:

You were willing to work extra hours during the bad weather last week. Thanks for your extra effort.

Presented to: *Diane Thompson*   Work site: *Riverside House*

Presented by *Marvin Lock*   Date: *4/6/95*

An important point to keep in mind when preparing written feedback using a standardized form such as the "Commendation Award" is to ensure the form allows for individualization of the written feedback. Nothing could appear more insincere than to receive a note of commendation only to find out several other people in the agency received the same feedback, duplicated exactly down to the last word. Relatedly, the form must be carefully prepared. Imagine a staff member's reaction to receiving a "Commendation Award" from a senior manager with the staff member's name misspelled — an occurrence we and others have observed on a number of occasions. Such practices can ruin an otherwise powerfully reinforcing experience for staff.

When written feedback requires more detail than can be provided on a simple form like the "Commendation Award", a form can be tailored for providing written feedback regarding a specific area of staff performance. The form presented on the following page was developed for giving feedback to staff concerning their teaching skills in school programs for students with severe developmental disabilities. Prior to routine use of the form, staff are trained to:

1. Always follow the order of teaching steps listed in a respective student's program

2. Use a specific strategy to prompt program steps a student does not independently attempt to complete

3. Provide reinforcement for any correctly completed step

4. Implement a specific error correction strategy when a student incorrectly completes a step

When prepared in this manner, the form directs or reminds the supervisor to give both positive and corrective feedback regarding each critical component of the staff person's teaching performance. The form also supplies space for indicating what future observations will entail so the staff member will know what will happen next (see Chapter 4), and prompts the supervisor to write a positive or encouraging comment at the end.

EXAMPLE OF A CHECKLIST FORM FOR
PROVIDING WRITTEN FEEDBACK

Evaluation of Client-Teaching Skills

Staff: _Susan Kessler_ Date: _3/1/95_ Observer: _Mary Porter_
Student: _Jackie_ Training Program: _hand washing_

(1) Steps Trained In Order
All Correct ✓ Errors __
Comments
_____
_____

(2) Prompts
All Correct__ Errors ✓
Comments
Start with a less intrusive prompt than
a physical prompt on steps 3 and 5.

(3) Reinforcement
All Correct ✓ Errors __
Comments
_____
_____

(4) Prompts
All Correct__ Errors ✓
Comments
Give Jackie more help on the 2nd trial
of steps when she makes errors.

Second observation of same training program necessary?
Yes ✓ No __
If yes, date of second observation will be _March 3rd._ If no, you will be notified when future observations are necessary.

General comments: _You are doing a nice job teaching this skill. Jackie is_ _already showing improvement._

Performance checklists similar to the form just described are quite useful for reducing the effort associated with providing detailed written feedback on a specific aspect of staff performance. As indicated in Chapter 3, performance checklists are also a useful tool for delineating and monitoring staff performance. In the latter cases, following the monitoring of staff performance the completed checklist can be given to staff as written feedback. The reader is referred to Chapter 3 for more discussion and examples of performance checklists.

Graphic Feedback. Another means of providing feedback is to numerically quantify information about staff performance and present the information to staff in graphic form. For example, a case manager in a psychiatric hospital could be given a bar graph showing the average number of admission forms she completed correctly each month. Such a graph could also show the average number completed correctly by her colleagues. The graph provides a picture of the case manager's performance compared to the performance of all case managers at the hospital.

An advantage of graphic feedback is it allows staff to compare their individual performance to a goal or standard for acceptable performance. To illustrate, a necessary component of a therapeutic environment in group homes for clients with serious physical disabilities is that the environment is enriched with things for the clients to do during leisure times. In such homes, staff are often responsible for ensuring leisure materials are within clients' reach as part of the environmental enrichment process. An agency's standard may be that at least 80% of clients will have leisure materials within arm's reach during designated leisure times. By graphing the percentage of clients with leisure materials within arm's reach observed in each home across several weeks, a supervisor can readily determine in which homes staff are achieving the standard as well as in which homes staff need more supervisory action to conform with the standard.

Graphic feedback can also provide a picture of an individual's current performance compared to his past performance. By comparing current performance to past performance, a staff member can quickly visualize whether or not his performance is improving or deteriorating. Graphs depicting performance over time are also a valuable source of information for supervisors. Such graphs allow supervisors to readily evaluate effects of any management practice they have implemented to improve specific aspects of staff performance. For example, a supervisor in a day care center may notice a teacher's assistant is rarely implementing activities listed on the lesson plan. The supervisor may address the situation first by observing the assistant's performance several times a day and noting whether the assistant is following the lesson plan (defined as conducting the activity at the time designated on the lesson plan). The supervisor can then graph the percentage of the total number of observations for which the assistant was following the lesson plan each day. After several days the supervisor may review the graph, and notice that on each day the assistant was ob served following the lesson plan less than half the designated time. The supervisor could then implement a strategy to improve the assistant's compliance with the lesson plan. The strategy could be, for example, to continue the frequent observations of the staff member and additionally, comment positively on the assistant's performance each time he is observed following the lesson plan. The supervisor will know if her supervisory strategy is effective if the graph shows a subsequent increase in the staff member's compliance with the lesson plan. If the positive comments did not improve the assistant's performance as reflected on the graph, the supervisor could try some other supervisory strategy. Such an objective analysis of the effectiveness of a management strategy allows supervisors to quickly dispense with ineffective procedures and continue a procedure found to actually improve the problematic performance.

In contrast to the advantages of graphic feedback, this type of feedback also shares many of the disadvantages of other forms of written feedback. In particular, the effort and time required of a supervisor to prepare and continuously update graphs can be rather considerable. Preparation time may become less of a disadvantage as human service agencies obtain computer equipment and software programs for constructing graphs more quickly and easily relative to traditional hand-made graphs. A second disadvantage specific to graphic feedback, however, can be more difficult to overcome than reducing preparation effort. That is, many direct service staff are unaccustomed to reading graphs. Such staff may be unable to accurately interpret the information represented in the graph without significant explanation from the supervisor. The compelling advantages of graphic feedback must be weighed against these disadvantages before routinely using graphs as a mechanism for providing feedback to staff.

Videotaped Feedback. One of the more elaborate means of providing feedback on previous work performance is by having staff view a videotape showing their actual performance in selected situations. A distinct advantage of providing feedback through videotapes is staff view their own performance moment-by-moment, just as a supervisor has observed the performance. Through videotape a staff member in a half-way house can, for example, actually see his interactions with a difficult-to-manage youth during group sharing time rather than trying to recall each interaction based on a supervisor's vocal description. Videotaped feedback provided in this manner typically represents the most detailed and accurate descriptive information about performance relative to all feedback mechanisms.

Despite the informative advantage of videotaped feedback, this type of feedback is the least utilized of all feedback mechanisms in human service agencies. The lack of utilization of videotaped feedback is due to two reasons. First, videotaped feedback is usually the most effortful and expensive of all feedback mechanisms for supervisors. In order to videotape staff performance supervisors must arrange to be in the work setting at a time when the target performance is likely to occur and arrange a subsequent time for the staff member to view the videotape. Videotaped feedback, of course, also requires the availability of a camera, tape, VCR, etc. However, even though the effort required for using videotaped feedback is relatively great, videotaped feedback still might be more widely utilized if not for the second disadvantage: staff often hate to be videotaped. Knowing a camera is recording every move makes many staff self-conscious and uncomfortable. Viewing oneself on videotape also can be somewhat embarrassing for staff. In short, videotaped feedback frequently is not very acceptable to staff. Because videotaped feedback is one of the least acceptable forms of feedback for staff, supervisors should consider using it with caution.

Combinations of Feedback Mechanisms. One way supervisors can capitalize on the advantages and counteract some of the disadvantages associated with particular feedback mechanisms is by combining feedback formats. For instance, vocal feedback can be combined with written feedback to capture the advantages of a face-to-face interaction associated with vocal feedback and the permanent record resulting from written feedback. Vocal feedback likewise can be provided in combination with graphic feedback to increase the likelihood staff understand the information depicted in the graphic representation.

Combining feedback mechanisms is often the most effective way to bring about positive changes in staff performance. Of course, the more feedback mechanisms used simultaneously by a supervisor, the greater the time and effort required of the supervisor to provide the feedback. Supervisors must weigh the advantages of combining feedback mechanisms with the disadvantage of increased time and effort. Other factors to consider in determining which feedback mechanism to use in a given situation include how comfortable the supervisor is in using various types of feedback mechanisms, which feedback mechanisms have worked most effectively in the past (based on a supervisor's review of the results of monitoring staff performance — Chapter 3), and which mechanisms staff seem to like the most. Given the wide array of specific formats for providing feedback, there are many feedback options available to supervisors who take a sincere interest in enhancing the work effort and enjoyment of their staff.

PROVIDING FEEDBACK THROUGH MULTIPLE MECHANISMS IS A VERY POWERFUL WAY FOR SUPERVISORS TO HELP STAFF IMPROVE THEIR WORK PERFORMANCE

Private Versus Public Feedback

In addition to the specific mechanism for providing feedback, feedback can be delivered either privately or publicly. In private feedback presentations, only the individual whose performance is being addressed has access to the information. When feedback is presented publicly, other members of the agency also are aware of the feedback given to an individual. Telling a staff member she has done an excellent job of arranging community support services for a client when no other staff are present is an example of private vocal feedback. The same feedback provided to the individual during a meeting with other staff present is an example of public vocal feedback. Written and graphic feedback can also be delivered either privately or publicly. Methods of privately providing written and graphic feedback were presented earlier. The following example demonstrates a means of providing written feedback in a public manner. This particular approach has been used in school programs serving students with special needs. Noteworthy performance by any teacher can be described on the written form by the school principal, and publicly posted in the lobby of the school for others to see.

EXAMPLE OF A FORMAT FOR PROVIDING PUBLIC WRITTEN FEEDBACK

A ROUND OF APPLAUSE FOR...!!!

Rita and Joe in Classroom #6—All their students passed at least one training program this month. Way to go guys!

PLEASE POST

Publicly conveying feedback can be a very powerful consequence for staff work performance. By making other staff members aware of an individual's commendable performance, the supervisor sets the occasion for positive feedback to be provided by others in addition to the supervisor. In the example just noted, other teachers at the school will see the posted information about the respective teacher's accomplishment and they too may congratulate the teacher. As a result, reinforcing interactions for the identified teacher occur multiple times during the days following public posting of the feedback.

The characteristic of public feedback which makes it most reinforcing (i.e., others are aware of the accomplishment and provide additional feedback) can also be the most serious drawback to public feedback. Receiving attention from one's colleagues is not reinforcing to everyone. Some individuals actually detest being in the spotlight and are embarrassed by the extra attention generated by public feedback, even when the attention is genuinely positive. An even worse scenario is when public feedback precipitates more than just unwanted positive attention from others. In this regard, a supervisor cannot control the type of attention staff receive from their colleagues as a result of the supervisor's publicly posted comments. Publicly posted praise, for example, may result in the staff member receiving negative comments when peers tease him about his accomplishment or accuse him of "brown nosing" the supervisor.

There are two ways to minimize the likelihood of unpleasant consequences resulting from public feedback. One way is to publicly present information about a group of staff members rather than highlighting the performance of only one individual. To illustrate, when all of the teacher assistants from the third grade are publicly recognized for developing a schedule for reading tutors, the focus of public attention falls on the whole group and not just one individual. Of course, when giving feedback to a group, a supervisor must be confident the performance of each group member deserves praise. If the performance of some group members was not praiseworthy, the supervisor will be, in effect, reinforcing undesirable performance among certain staff by complimenting the group's work (see earlier discussion in this chapter of consequence mistakes).

A second way the advantages of public feedback can be captured while minimizing the possible disadvantages is to publicly post information pertaining to client welfare. Although indicators of client welfare are correlated with some aspect of staff performance, the publicly posted information on client welfare is not a direct reflection per se on any one staff member's performance. For instance, a supervisor in a nursing home might post a graph showing a reduction in bedtime toileting accidents since evening shift staff began assisting clients to go to the bathroom before bedtime. Posting information on client welfare not only removes the focus of attention away from individual staff, it also refocuses attention on why improving staff performance is an issue in the first place — it impacts client welfare.

At the same time, important information is provided to staff pertaining to how well they have performed a particular job task. Of course, client confidentiality issues should always be kept in mind when client welfare indicators are being considered to be part of public feedback presentations.

Related to the advantages and disadvantages of providing public feedback is one hard and fast rule: Never publicly provide negative feedback. Staff can easily become embarrassed or even humiliated when negative feedback is purposefully made public. Not only will the staff who receive the feedback likely be severely punished, those staff who witness such feedback will often feel uncomfortable. Staff who observe one of their peers seriously criticized in public by the supervisor usually believe the supervisor is acting very inappropriately, and can lose respect for the supervisor.

WHEN NEGATIVE OR CRITICAL FEEDBACK IS NECESSARY TO IMPROVE STAFF PERFORMANCE, THE FEEDBACK SHOULD BE PRESENTED INDIVIDUALLY AND PRIVATELY

How Frequently Should Feedback Be Provided?

How frequently performance feedback should be provided depends primarily on how well or poorly staff are performing. When staff competently perform a duty on a routine basis, feedback is needed less frequently than when staff are not performing as competently as the supervisor expects. Consistent observations of staff performance will indicate about how often feedback is needed to obtain and/or maintain an adequate level of staff performance.

Although the best indicator of how frequently feedback should be provided is the adequacy of staff performance, there are certain circumstances in which staff will almost always require frequent feedback to ensure adequate performance. In particular, supervisors should be prepared to provide frequent feedback — such as at least several times a week — when staff have recently learned a work skill and are expected to perform the new skill as part of the routine job. As discussed in Chapter 4, in many agencies staff training is conducted in classroom settings and not in the work setting where use of the new work skill will ultimately be required. In these cases frequent feedback will be necessary in the regular work environment until staff consistently perform the skill correctly on the day-to-day job.

Another situation in which staff often require frequent feedback is when staff are required to change long-standing work routines. When a teacher's primary method of teaching for years has been group instruction and seatwork assignments, for example, a change to activity center-based instruction will require frequent feedback from the supervisor to help the teacher adequately develop the new work habits. Similarly, when new performance expectations require substantially more effort on the part of staff relative to previous performance expectations, feedback will be needed frequently until staff grow accustomed to the new and more effortful routine. For instance, a supervisor in a rest home can expect to give frequent performance feedback when she initially requires staff to engage clients in leisure activities as well as provide personal care when previously only personal care duties had been required of the staff.

A final situation requiring frequent feedback is when supervisors find other sources of feedback are competing with their supervisory feedback to affect staff performance in undesirable ways. Clients, client guardians, staff from other agencies, professional staff and the staff member's coworkers all represent potential sources of feedback. Sometimes feedback provided from the latter sources is discrepant from the staff supervisor's feedback. To illustrate, a staff member's diligent work with clients in a vocational program may be slowly declining even though the supervisor is giving the staff member positive feedback on a weekly basis concerning his good work. The decline in performance could be the result of critical feedback received from less motivated coworkers — coworkers who resent their colleague's hard work efforts because it makes the coworkers look bad. If positive supervisory feedback is provided frequently during such situations, it is more likely to successfully compete with the resentment and negative feedback from coworkers relative to supervisory feedback provided infrequently.

SUPERVISORY FEEDBACK SHOULD BE ESPECIALLY FREQUENT WHEN:

1. Staff first incorporate a new skill into their work routine
2. Changes are required in long-standing work routines
3. New performance expectations result in substantial increases in work effort relative to the current performance expectations
4. Other sources of feedback threaten to change staff performance in undesirable ways

Although answering the question regarding how frequently feedback should be given depends on a number of factors as just illustrated, one factor is certain. As long as performance feedback is positive and follows desirable work performance, there is really no danger of giving too much.

Enhancing the Power of Supervisory Feedback

As stressed in the beginning of this chapter, most staff members view their supervisor's appraisal of their work as important and will try to perform their work duties to their supervisor's satisfaction. For these staff members, supervisory feedback is a very powerful management tool. Sooner or later though, every supervisor will encounter staff who will not regard supervisory feedback as very important and will not respond to feedback with improved performance. Regardless of the feedback mechanism or frequency, feedback alone will not be effective in improving the performance of these individuals. For such staff, a supervisor must find ways to enhance the effectiveness of her feedback. One way to enhance feedback effectiveness is to combine the feedback with other types of consequences which are already valuable to respective staff. By consistently pairing feedback with positive consequences that are already meaningful to staff, a supervisor's feedback in and of itself will eventually be valued by the staff. Chapter 8 discusses in more detail strategies for enhancing the value of supervisory feedback.

SECTION 3

ENHANCING WORK ENJOYMENT

Chapter 6

ENHANCING OVERALL WORK ENJOYMENT: INCREASING THE GOOD THINGS IN STAFFS' WORK ENVIRONMENT

In Chapter 2 it was stressed when there is lack of motivation among an agency's staff, the primary problem is the agency is not providing a motivating work environment for staff. Correspondingly, in such situations it is the supervisor's job to take active steps to make the environment more motivating. This chapter presents strategies to ensure the overall work environment of a human service agency is indeed highly motivating. However, whereas Chapters 3 - 5 focused on the work diligence and competence aspects of motivation, this chapter focuses on the enjoyment staff experience while performing their jobs. The strategies to be discussed are designed to transform an unmotivating environment, or one in which there is little work enjoyment, into a motivating environment in which staff clearly enjoy their day-to-day work situation. The strategies are also intended to help supervisors ensure a work environment that is already motivating in terms of work enjoyment maintains its motivating qualities for the agency's staff.

Maintaining a highly motivating work environment is a vital part of a supervisor's job often overlooked in human service agencies. When agency staff are working diligently and seem to be enjoying their work, supervisors generally assume motivation is not an issue in their respective agencies. Such an assumption can be devastating for the agency's long-term effectiveness — staff motivation is not a static phenomenon. As indicated in Chapter 2, often new employees enter an agency being highly motivated to work but soon lose their motivation because the work environment is not supportive of diligent and enjoyable work habits. Relatedly, a motivating work environment at one point in time may not have motivating properties at a future point in time even though the work environment remains the same over the given time period. The latter situation occurs because the work environment, no matter how conducive to enjoyable and diligent work habits, can become routinized for staff; staff become accustomed to the environment and what was previously exciting and motivating for staff becomes repetitive and monotonous. Hence, a supervisor must implement specific strategies to turn an unmotivating work environment into a motivating one, and to maintain a work environment that is already highly motivating.

WHEN A WORK ENVIRONMENT IS CURRENTLY HIGHLY MOTIVATING FOR STAFF, THE SUPERVISOR'S JOB IS TO WORK ACTIVELY TO MAINTAIN THAT ENVIRONMENT

In order to successfully implement the motivational strategies discussed in this chapter, a basic tenet should be accepted by supervisors: doing things to enhance staff motivation must be an ongoing part of supervisors' day-to-day job duties. Implementing motivational strategies should be a part of a supervisor's "to-do" list just like any other routine supervisory job, be it establishing staff work schedules, responding to unexpected staff absences, completing administrative reports, or returning phone calls. Supervisors should ask themselves on a routine basis the simple question, "What have I done to help my staff work hard and enjoy their work?". The more often supervisors can answer this question by acknowledging specific things they have done, the more likely it is their staff will be working in a highly motivating job environment.

SUPERVISORS SHOULD FREQUENTLY ASK THEMSELVES "WHAT HAVE I DONE TO HELP MY STAFF WORK HARD AND ENJOY THEIR WORK?"

Using Performance Consequences to Enhance Staff Enjoyment With the Daily Work Environment

In the previous section of this book, the important role of positive consequences for increasing and maintaining desirable work performance of staff was stressed. It was also emphasized to use positive consequences effectively, supervisors should ensure: (a) desired job responsibilities of staff are clearly defined in terms of specific work behaviors, (b) identified duties are monitored frequently and objectively to ensure the duties are being fulfilled and, (c) positive consequences are provided based on observed fulfillment of expected work responsibilities. The same general process can be used to enhance the amount of enjoyment staff experience in the overall work environment. However, there are also some important differences between using performance consequences to affect daily work performance and to affect enjoyment within the work environment at large.

The primary difference between using performance consequences for increasing and maintaining highly specified work performances on a daily basis versus making the work environment consistently enjoyable from an overall perspective is twofold. First, to enhance overall work enjoyment, positive consequences do not need to be provided contingent on specific work behaviors on a daily or otherwise very frequent basis. General work enjoyment of staff can be enhanced by providing positive consequences based on more global indices of desirable staff performance, and on a less frequent basis. Second, for impacting the work environment overall, the performance consequences need to be of a more novel and generally more special nature relative to the consequences provided on a day-to-day or week-to-week basis. These differences between enhancing desirable work performance on a routine basis and making the overall agency environment an enjoyable one will be elaborated on as this chapter progresses.

Before active steps can be taken to ensure staff enjoy their work, what actually constitutes an enjoyable work environment must be broken down into specific work characteristics and practices. In this regard, it should be realized in any work environment there are things staff enjoy and things staff do not enjoy. Simply put, there are good things and bad things in every work environment. Supervisors must determine, through their observations and interactions with staff, precisely what constitutes those good and bad things. Subsequently, the supervisor's job is to increase the good things for staff and decrease the bad things. We like to paraphrase this aspect of a supervisor's job simply as increasing the goods and decreasing the bad. When the good things occurring in the work environment far outnumber the bad things, staff will find the work environment enjoyable.

**ENJOYABLE WORK ENVIRONMENT =
MORE GOOD THINGS HAPPENING FOR
STAFF THAN BAD THINGS**

The process of increasing the good things for staff in the work place and decreasing the bad things is simple to conceptualize but often difficult for supervisors to accomplish. In particular, for reasons to be explained later it is often easier and more pleasant for supervisors to increase the goods than to decrease the bad. Again though, both aspects must be addressed if supervisors are to successfully establish and maintain an enjoyable work environment for their staff. This chapter focuses on the first aspect, that of increasing the good things in staffs' work environment. Chapter 7 addresses decreasing the bad.

The Ultimate Goal for Establishing An Enjoyable Work Environment

As indicated in Chapter 2, staff generally work most diligently if they have a work goal to strive to obtain. Likewise, the work performance of supervisors is enhanced if supervisors have certain work goals to direct their efforts. Hence, if a significant component of a supervisor's job is to implement strategies to establish and maintain an enjoyable work life for staff, it would be beneficial for supervisors to have a goal to work toward in this area. We have found a useful goal, albeit an ambitious one, for enhancing staffs' work enjoyment is to arrange work conditions such that staff get up in the morning and look forward to going to work.

We have presented the goal for staff work enjoyment as just noted to numerous staff in human service agencies around the United States and the most common response from staff is one of general amusement. Many personnel in the human services laugh at such a proposal — the idea of work life being something to routinely look forward to is simply a foreign concept. In one sense, the rather skeptical view human service personnel have of this concept being realistic is a sad commentary on the level of staff motivation existing in many human service agencies. Readers of this text can relate to the concept by asking themselves how often they actually get up in the morning and truly look forward to going to work. Hopefully, many readers can answer the question affirmatively in that they usually do like going to work. A more probable response of readers though is that sometimes they look forward to going to work. The supervisor's task is to change the "sometimes" type of response among their staff to at least an "almost always" response.

SUPERVISORY GOAL FOR ESTABLISHING AND MAINTAINING AN ENJOYABLE WORK ENVIRONMENT: STAFF WILL GET UP EACH MORNING AND LOOK FORWARD TO GOING TO WORK

Enhancing Work Enjoyment: Strategies for Increasing The Good Things In Staffs' Work Environment

The strategies discussed in the following sections represent different approaches supervisors can use to enhance the enjoyment staff experience with their work. Some strategies may appeal to different supervisors more than others. Some strategies may also be counterindicated in some agencies due to union contracts, agency policy, etc. Nevertheless, we have found most of the approaches can be implemented in typical human service agencies in one form or another. The primary point, which has been stressed repeatedly, is supervisors must actively take steps to make the work environment enjoyable for staff. The following strategies are meant to provide supervisors with ideas for those steps. Dedicated supervisors will undoubtedly expand on the strategies to be discussed by using their own creativity and resource availability.

Special Recognition Activities

As the examples to be presented in this section will indicate, special recognition activities represent events many human service agencies currently have in place (as well as events many for-profit organizations in the nonhuman service work sector have in place). Generally, these events are designed to recognize and/or provide some type of observable award for especially notable achievements of staff. The approaches represent an effective means of periodically enhancing staff's enjoyment with the work environment.

Before describing special recognition activities, an important qualification is warranted regarding the overall effectiveness of these types of activities. Managerial personnel sometimes assume special recognition activities will help staff perform their jobs better on a day-to-day basis. This assumption is typically erroneous. Special recognition activities usually occur too infrequently to significantly affect a staff person's daily work performance. As discussed in Chapter 5, to impact how a staff person performs routinely, performance consequences must be provided very frequently, and usually at least daily or weekly.

A second reason special recognition activities cannot be relied on to affect daily performance is the activities typically are based on a staff person's overall performance and not on clearly specified and monitored work behaviors. Again as discussed in Chapter 5, consequences must be contingent on clearly delineated work behaviors if the consequences are to increase or maintain those behaviors. In short, it should not be assumed special recognition activities will improve or maintain daily work performance. These activities can be used periodically though to help staff persons feel good about the work place. Feeling good about the work place represents one type of good thing in staffs' work environment and consequently, something super-visors should strive to help staff achieve.

The examples to follow are some of the more popular spe-cial recognition activities used in human service agencies. Al-though the activities are presented separately, they also can be used in combination. When considering these activities either singularly or in combination, it should be stressed although the activities are presented based on work performance from a glo-bal perspective, they are still based on performance. To en-hance staff motivation, special recognition activities must be based on actual performance accomplishments of staff.

It is also important the reasons a staff person receives spe-cial recognition be clearly articulated in terms of performance-based accomplishments. Many if not all staff in the agency will be aware of the individual who receives special recognition, and those staff need to know it is what the person accomplished in the work place that is being rewarded. If the reasons are based on factors other than performance-based accomplishments, such as because an agency executive likes a respective staff person due to his attractiveness or friendliness with the execu-tive, the overall impact on staff motivation can be most detri-mental (see Chapter 7 for explanation of how such a process can actually increase bad things happening to staff). A similar outcome results if the reasons for the special recognition are not specified publicly in terms of performance-based accom-plishments. In the latter situation, staff are left to determine for themselves why a respective staff member received special rec-ognition, and staff may not make accurate assumptions.

SPECIAL RECOGNITION ACTIVITIES SHOULD BE PROVIDED BASED ON STAFFS' PERFORMANCE ACCOMPLISHMENTS AND THE REASON FOR THE RECOGNITION SHOULD BE KNOWN BY ALL STAFF

When the problematic situations just noted are avoided and special recognition activities are indeed based on well articulated, performance-related accomplishments, the recognition activities can make staff feel quite good about the work place. When provided appropriately, special recognition activities can also serve as a positive incentive for other staff to strive to achieve various work-related accomplishments. The latter outcome occurs because staff become aware hard work is valued by management and those staff increase their work efforts to obtain recognition for their work accomplishments.

Special Recognition Awards. Probably the most common type of special recognition activity is accomplishment awards. A number of agencies have developed "Employee of The Year" or "Employee of The Month" types of award systems. These kinds of awards can also be more specific to various types of staff positions such as "Teacher Aide of The Year" or "Group Home Parent of The Year". Alternatively, the awards can be identified more by the type of accomplishment than by the type of staff position in the agency. Examples of the latter awards include "Outstanding Client Trainer Award", "Perfect Attendance Award" and "Advocacy Effectiveness Award". Typically these types of awards are presented at a special ceremony such as an all-staff banquet and are accompanied by presentation of a recognition plaque or certificate. Somewhat less formal but nonetheless special processes for presenting the awards entail a group of supervisors or senior executives meeting with the staff recipient in the latter's work place or during a routine staff meeting to present the award in front of the recipient's work peers.

When using special recognition awards, a nice touch can be to follow the award presentation with a summary in the local newspaper of the award and why it was given to the staff member. Presenting the information in the newspaper has the effect of enhancing the value of the award to the receiving staff member because the staff person's friends, family members, neighbors, etc., may read the information and personally congratulate the staff member. When other people in the staff person's life provide congratulations, the amount of recognition the staff person receives for a job well done is increased noticeably relative to if the recognition comes only during the official award presentation.

Special Privileges. Another type of special recognition activity frequently used in human service agencies is to award staff with special privileges. Special privileges are used similarly to awards except the recognition is not typically provided during a special ceremony but rather, through a less formal announcement. Also, the outcome of the recognition is that for a designated period of time, the staff person whose performance accomplishments are being recognized is provided with certain desirable, work-related privileges not usually available in the work place. The basic intent of the privileges is to make the work environment a little bit nicer for the employee due to her work accomplishments.

Using work privileges not routinely available as a means of enhancing the enjoyment in the work place provides a nice example of the process described earlier of increasing the good things and decreasing the bad things in a staff person's work environment. For example, something many staff like — and therefore a good thing to be increased in the work environment

— is the opportunity to work a flex schedule each week. A flexible work week allows a staff member to determine (within reasonable limits) exactly when she will work her 40 hours, or some portion thereof. Having a flexible work schedule is often attractive to staff because it allows a staff person to arrange the work schedule around her personal or family schedule. A flexible work schedule is usually a special privilege because most agencies cannot allow many staff to have a large degree of control over their work schedule because specified numbers of staff must be at work at certain times to provide the agency's services. However, flexible work privileges are frequently granted to administrative and upper eschelon personnel in human service agencies. Supervisors can extend the same type of privilege to direct service staff where possible, even if the privilege involves simply coming to work 30 minutes later than usual, to enhance the latter staffs' enjoyment with their work routine.

In contrast to providing a flexible work schedule as a means of increasing the good things in a staff person's work environment, an example of a privilege intended to reduce the bad things is to relieve a staff person of a work duty the staff member does not like to perform. To illustrate, in one congregate care facility for people with profound developmental disabilities with which we have consulted, an activity rated by staff as one of the most desirable work privileges was to be relieved of having to feed lunch to people who could not feed themselves due to physical disabilities. In this case, the staff person whose performance accomplishments were being recognized was relieved of lunch time duties by having the staff supervisor periodically fill in for the staff member to conduct the latter's feeding duties. Additional types of privileges used to decrease undesirable things in a staff person's work life are described in Chapter 7.

As with special awards, there are a number of different types of special privileges (in addition to those already noted) that can be used to provide something enjoyable for a staff person. Listed below are some of the more common privileges supervisors in human service agencies have used as special recognition activities. Of course, not every privilege exemplified below will be desirable for all staff. Supervisors must be cognizant of the fact different staff have different likes and dislikes. It is incumbent upon supervisors to determine what types of privileges each staff person most desires.

WORK PRIVILEGES USED BY SUPERVISORS AS SPECIAL RECOGNITION ACTIVITIES

- easily accessible parking spaces
- working on novel, special projects
- paid travel to conferences
- directing special agency functions
- having control over certain monies for purchasing personal items for clients
- paid leave time for special recreational outings with clients

Informal Recognition

Whereas the strategies discussed to this point generally involve rather formal processes, there are many important things a supervisor can do on an informal or impromptu basis to enhance the overall enjoyment in a staff person's work life. Actually, the less formal, good things supervisors can do for staff usually have more of an impact on overall work enjoyment on a day-to-day basis than the formal, special recognition activities. The less formal strategies, as discussed in this section, are especially important because they can be provided much more frequently than the more formal activities. Relatedly, the less formal recognition activities can be provided to a larger number of staff persons at a given point in time than the latter activities. Also, the less formal supervisory procedures often are viewed by staff as a more sincere recognition of staffs' performance accomplishments. In order to frequently implement procedures on an informal or impromptu basis to enhance staffs' overall work enjoyment, a general guideline should be followed: supervisors should continuously be on the lookout for staff who are doing a nice job. Subsequently, supervisors should strive to do good things for staff based on the observed performance. The following sections describe some of the good things supervisors can do in this regard.

SUPERVISORS SHOULD CONTINUOUSLY BE ON THE LOOKOUT TO CATCH STAFF DOING A NICE JOB

Frequent, Impromptu Praise. The importance of positive feedback for improving specific work performances was highlighted in Chapter 5. The same type of positive comments can be used on an informal and impromptu basis to increase staffs' overall work enjoyment. As just alluded to, the first step in the process is for supervisors to continuously look for praiseworthy aspects of respective staff members' work performance. When such aspects are observed, supervisors can immediately commend the staff for the desirable performance. For particularly special recognition, praise statements can also be provided in a delayed fashion later in the work day or week. Actually, in some cases delayed praise can have a more positive effect on staff than if the supervisor had immediately praised the observed performance. With delayed praise, staff often are aware the supervisor must have been quite pleased with the observed performance because the supervisor made special efforts to come to the staffs' work site at a later point in time just to commend the staffs' previous performance.

Saying Good Things Behind Someone's Back. One of the most unpleasant social behaviors in terms of negative impact on people is to gossip or say bad things about a person when the person is not present. This socially undesirable but frequent practice in our society can be turned around by supervisors as a means of increasing the nicer qualities in a staff person's work life — supervisors can say good things about a staff person's performance when the staff person is not present.

Complimenting a staff member's performance when the staff person is not around can have two desirable outcomes for enhancing staff motivation. First, often the individual whose performance is complimented to other staff will hear about what the supervisor said through the informal work grapevine. When staff hear about the comments, the staff usually feel good about what was said. Again, feeling good about something in the work place adds one more good thing in the staff person's overall work environment. Second, the performance of staff who hear a supervisor compliment a staff person's performance when the staff person is not present can also be beneficially affected. The supervisor's comments can function as a positive incentive for those staff to perform in the same manner as the identified staff person (i.e., to work hard and/or proficiently). Of course, if the supervisor's praise comments are to function as an incentive to the other staff, the staff must value the supervisor's opinion and attention. As noted previously, most staff do value the supervisor's opinion, if for no other reason than the fact the supervisor can have a significant impact on staffs' job permanency.

SUPERVISORS SHOULD STRIVE TO SAY GOOD THINGS ABOUT PERFORMANCE BEHIND A STAFF PERSON'S BACK

Taking Home the Goods. An ideal time to compliment a staff person's performance is just before the staff person leaves work, such as the end of the work day. More relevant from a motivational standpoint, positive comments can be provided when the staff person is leaving work for an extended period such as just before the weekend or before a holiday or vacation.

Commending a staff person's performance immediately before he leaves work can have several beneficial effects for enhancing a staff person's work motivation. First, all the positive effects of praising work performance in general as discussed in this and preceding chapters can result. Second, the practice can have the effect of causing the staff person to focus on something good in the work place (i.e., the nice things the supervisor said to him) while the staff person is away from work. This effect is what we call taking home the goods.

Undoubtedly, many readers can recall just the opposite situation of taking home the goods, when something bad at work had a negative effect on them when they left work — in essence, taking home the bad. The latter process results in staff complaining to spouses or friends about unpleasant aspects of work or simply going home in a bad mood. Often, when staff think about the bad aspects of their jobs away from work, they tend to ruminate on those bad aspects. The continued reflecting on the bad aspects can have the effect of increasing the negative impact of those aspects on staffs' overall enjoyment with work. Probably the worse case scenario is when staff have trouble sleeping at night because they are very disturbed about bad or unpleasant things at work and cannot get those things out of their mind. Not only do these situations cause unpleasantness for people, they also can cause staff to be reluctant to return to work or to skip work altogether. In any case, staff are more likely to return to work with a bad mind set about their job. In turn, when staff return to work feeling bad about the job, work enjoyment usually suffers, making the supervisor's job of motivating staff most difficult.

Hopefully readers will also have had the experience of focusing on good things about their job while away from work. Supervisors can help in this respect by making sincere efforts to catch staff before they leave work and explicitly commend staff for their work performance. Such a practice has the opposite result of that just described when staff go home feeling bad about their job. Leaving work just after having been sincerely complimented for work performance can help staff think about something good in the work place, reduce unpleasantness at home due to the job, and make staff more pleased about going back to work.

Involving Staff in Decision Making

Strategies discussed to this point for enhancing work enjoyment have focused on specific actions supervisors can take to increase the good things in staffs' work environment. There are other strategies to enhance work enjoyment involving specific actions staff members themselves can take. The latter steps also involve supervisory actions, but the intent of the actions is not to enhance staff work enjoyment directly, but to enhance enjoyment indirectly by increasing staffs' control over the good things in their work environment. Supervisors can assist staff in enhancing their own work enjoyment through processes of participative management.

Various forms of participative management historically have peaked and waned in popularity among managerial personnel in both the human service and nonhuman service work fields. Although there have been numerous labels given to participative management strategies over the years, the common link among all the approaches is they actively involve staff in controlling important aspects of their work environment. Our concern here is not to describe the various approaches to participative management, but rather, to simply describe what supervisors specifically can do to allow staff to influence the good things happening in their work environment.

SUPERVISORS CAN ENHANCE STAFF WORK ENJOYMENT BY ALLOWING STAFF TO HAVE CONTROL OVER EVENTS AFFECTING STAFFS' WORK LIFE

Before describing specific actions supervisors can take to involve staff in the management of their work place — which in essence serves to empower staff — two qualifications about participative management in general warrant mention. First, there has been considerable controversy over whether participative management strategies result in more diligent work performance among staff relative to management strategies in which staff have little if any formal involvement (i.e., work place management is essentially under the total control of supervisors or senior executive personnel). Our review of the research on participative management suggests such strategies do not necessarily result in more diligent work efforts among staff. The research does indicate, along with our own experience, staff tend to like participative approaches more than management strategies in which they have little involvement. Hence, involving staff in the management of their work place represents another good thing supervisors can provide within staffs' work routine.

The second qualification regarding participative management strategies is, contrary to some popularized notions in the management literature, these approaches to staff supervision do not represent panaceas for resolving problems with staff motivation. For one thing, some motivational problems have nothing to do with the degree to which staff are involved in managerial decision making. More importantly however, whereas some staff enjoy being heavily involved in the management of their work place, some staff do not enjoy such involvement. The degree to which supervisors actively involve respective staff in work place management should be based on each supervisor's determination of how much particular staff like to be involved in managerial activities. Attempts to involve all staff in participative management endeavors will undoubtedly result in some staff doing something they do not want to do, with a subsequent negative impact on the latter staffs' work enjoyment. For those staff who do like involvement in managerial activities, the following strategies represent means through which the staff can be actively involved in managing aspects of their work environment.

Participative Goal-Setting. As discussed in Chapter 3, the role of direct service staff in most human service agencies involves many types of work duties. Typically, it is up to the supervisor to determine which of those duties consititute the priority job responsibilities for staff to perform at a given point in time. In one sense, when a supervisor determines the priority job responsibilities for staff, the supervisor is establishing work goals for staff. An alternative means for establishing work goals or responsibilities is to allow staff to have input into what should constitute their priority work duties.

The process for involving staff in decisions regarding their priority work duties and related work goals is conceptually straightforward. In essence, the supervisor meets with staff, or various representatives of staff, and the group jointly decides the most important duties to fulfill during a designated time period. Of course, the ultimate decision regarding what must occur in the work place remains with the supervisor because that is a primary aspect of a supervisor's job. Using a participative management approach though, the supervisor's decision is significantly affected by what staff believe to be the most important job duties.

There are numerous areas in most human service settings in which staff can participate in deciding what the priority job duties should be, as well as other types of work goals. Involving staff in all decisions regarding work-related goals, however, is unrealistic because the process would be too time consuming and eventually counterproductive to actually getting all the jobs done. The supervisor must determine which decisions about work goals should be made with significant involvement of staff.

A useful guideline for determining job decisions in which to involve staff is that staff should have input in decisions affecting what staff perceive as the most important aspects of their jobs. One area of critical importance to staff is their overall work schedule, such as which days of the week they will be scheduled to work. In particular, in those agencies providing residential services (e.g., nursing homes, group homes, institutions), work schedules are especially important to staff because the schedules involve weekend work. Many staff do not like to work weekends due to personal and family reasons. Alot of direct service staff also moonlight by working jobs in addition to their human service job, and their work schedule in the human service agency affects how much they can moonlight. Consequently, allowing staff to have input in decisions such as how many weekends per month each staff person will work and which days during the week they will not be scheduled to work can be very rewarding to staff.

ALLOWING STAFF TO HAVE INPUT IN DECISIONS AFFECTING THE MOST IMPORTANT ASPECTS OF THEIR JOBS REPRESENTS A SIGNIFICANT MEANS OF INCREASING SOMETHING GOOD IN STAFFS' WORK LIFE

Participative Problem-Solving. A second area in which it can be rewarding for staff to be involved in managerial decision making pertains to solving problems in the work place from time to time. The process for involving staff in problem-solving activities is generally the same as the process for involving staff in goal setting: the supervisor meets with staff, obtains their input on how to solve a problem and then acts on the input. Also, the same general guideline regarding the problem areas in which to involve staff is relevant — staff should be involved in solving problems pertaining to aspects of staffs' jobs that staff view as particularly important. For example, a typical problem in human service agencies relating to the work schedule issue just noted is frequent absenteeism. Frequent absenteeism by certain staff has most unpleasant consequences for those staff who are at work. When staff are unexpectedly absent from work, the staff who are present may be "pulled" to other work areas to cover for the absent staff or must simply work harder to cover the workload of the absent staff. Each of these situations represents aspects of the work routine staff seriously dislike. Involving staff in determining how to reduce excessive staff absenteeism, such as identifying acceptable levels of absences as well as determining disciplinary consequences for staff who are frequently absent, can be rewarding for staff. Such involvement increases the likelihood whatever absentee-reduction procedures are implemented will be acceptable to staff relative to if the supervisor determines the procedures without significant staff input.

Money as A Motivator

Many people believe the most important motivator in the work place is money. Although whether or not money is indeed the most important motivator is subject to serious debate, clearly money can be one important source of motivation. People generally will increase their work effort to obtain more money and people typically enjoy their jobs more when they receive increased amounts of money relative to what they have previously been receiving. However, we do not focus on using money as a motivator for one primary reason: most supervisors in human service agencies are not able to frequently use money in a manner that would motivate people to work harder or better as described in Chapter 5. Use of money for staff work performance is usually under the control of senior agency executives or some small body of administrative personnel. Even senior executives in certain agencies do not have sufficient control over employee pay to use money as an effective motivator due to overriding agency policies or union contracts. Nevertheless, we offer a few suggestons for using money as a motivator because some agencies, and particularly agencies in the private sector, can have considerable control over employee pay. Also, someone in every human service agency has at least some control over money at least some of the time.

The most common use of money as a potential motivator in human service agencies rests with merit increases. As most readers are aware, merit pay represents one means by which an agency can provide a positive consequence for commendable or meritorious staff performance. When merit monies are indeed available within a human service agency, it is incumbent upon a supervisor to ensure the monies are distributed to staff in a motivating manner.

One difficulty in using pay as a motivator even when supervisors control how merit monies are disbursed is the infrequency with which merit monies are available to the agency. In most publicly operated agencies, for example, merit monies usually are available only once per year, and even the annual availability is not assured due to economic fluctuations in a respective agency's budget. To illustrate, we would guess many readers have experienced the situation of working for a county- or state-operated agency for consecutive years without having access to merit increases due to insufficient funds in their parent organization's budget. Nonetheless, if and when merit monies are available, guidelines should be followed if the monies are to be used as a means of enhancing the enjoyment staff experience in their work place.

Guidelines for using merit monies to enhance work enjoyment among staff are basically the same guidelines as those noted earlier regarding special recognition activities. First, the monies should be distributed to staff based solely on specific performance accomplishments. Distributing money based on performance accomplishments can be an easy process if the suggestions for defining and monitoring work performance as discussed in Chapter 3 are followed. Second, the fact merit monies are provided due to performance accomplishments should be well explained to all staff. If merit monies are not distributed based on performance accomplishments or staff do not know how the monies are dispensed, then all the negative effects on staff motivation as described with special recognition activities can result with the use of merit monies.

MERIT MONIES SHOULD BE DISTRIBUTED BASED ON PERFORMANCE-BASED ACCOMPLISHMENTS AND STAFF MUST BE INFORMED HOW THE MONIES ARE DISTRIBUTED

Chapter 7

ENHANCING OVERALL WORK ENJOYMENT: DECREASING THE BAD THINGS IN STAFFS' WORK ENVIRONMENT

In Chapter 6 it was stressed an enjoyable work environment exists for staff when more good things happen in the work place than bad things. It was also noted it is usually easier for supervisors, as part of their efforts to enhance work enjoyment, to increase the good things for staff than to decrease the bad. Decreasing those events and activities staff dislike about their job often involves work factors over which supervisors have little control. Also, as discussed later in this chapter, what supervisors must do to decrease certain negative things in their staffs' work environment are not always pleasant duties for supervisors. Nevertheless, if supervisors are to effectively enhance the enjoyment and related work motivation among staff, supervisors must routinely strive to decrease the negative events and activities in staffs' work environment. This chapter discusses strategies supervisors can use to decrease aspects of typical human service environments staff frequently dislike.

SUPERVISORS MUST ROUTINELY STRIVE TO DECREASE THE NEGATIVE ASPECTS OF STAFFS' WORK ENVIRONMENT

Before supervisors can effectively decrease the bad things in staffs' work environment, supervisors must determine those aspects staff dislike about the job, and particularly those things staff most seriously dislike. Making such determinations requires supervisors to carefully observe staff reactions to different events occurring in the routine work environment. Observations should include how staff act as well as what staff say in response to various job-related events. Hence, a vital skill for supervisors is to critically and sensitively observe staff behavior. Supervisors must observe staff reactions to what the supervisors do themselves as well as staff reactions to what other people (e.g., senior agency executives, other supervisors, other staff) do in the work place.

SUPERVISORS MUST CAREFULLY OBSERVE STAFF REACTIONS TO EVENTS AND ACTIVITIES IN THE WORK PLACE

Critically observing staff reactions to work events in order to determine what staff like and dislike about their jobs represents a supervision skill rarely addressed in supervisory training programs. As such, supervisors are typically left to their own means of determining how to identify staff likes and dislikes for different work events. Fortunately in this regard, there is one simple strategy supervisors can use to increase the likelihood of observing staff reactions to aspects of the work environment and determine staff likes and dislikes: ensure frequent interactions with staff. In essence, the more frequently a supervisor interacts with his staff, the more likely the supervisor will be aware of staffs' likes and dislikes.

Noting the importance of frequent work-related interactions between a supervisor and his staff appears to be stating the obvious. Few readers are likely to argue with the notion supervisors must interact frequently with their staff to effectively supervise staff job performance in general, much less to fulfill the motivational requirement of a supervisor's job. Nonetheless, we stress the point here because for a variety of reasons both legitimate and illegitimate, supervisors often become trapped in work situations in which they find themselves interacting quite infrequently with their staff. Probably the most common example is when supervisors spend excessive time in seemingly endless meetings with other supervisors or administrative personnel; time that could be spent with the supervisors' staff. Supervisors must be aware of when they become overly involved in administrative meetings and make concerted efforts to change their supervisory routines to ensure frequent interactions with staff.

FREQUENT INTERACTIONS WITH STAFF INCREASE THE LIKELIHOOD SUPERVISORS KNOW WHAT STAFF LIKE AND DISLIKE ABOUT THE JOB

In Chapter 3 the importance of supervisors formally monitoring job performance in staffs' regular work situation was stressed as one step for ensuring staff work proficiently and diligently. Routine on-the-job monitoring also affords supervisors opportunities to observe staff reactions to various work events and in turn, help supervisors determine those job aspects staff tend to dislike. In addition to formal monitoring of staff performance, there are a number of other types of opportunities for supervisors to observe staff reactions to various aspects of their work life. Listed on the following page are examples of some of the more opportune situations supervisors can use to make accurate determinations of staffs' dislikes about the job. In reviewing the examples, the primary point for supervisors to remember is that to increase staff work enjoyment by decreasing bad things in the work environment, supervisors should be consistently on the lookout for what constitutes bad things for staff.

OPPORTUNE TIMES FOR OBSERVING STAFF REACTIONS TO ASPECTS OF THE WORK ENVIRONMENT AS A MEANS OF DETERMINING STAFF DISLIKES ABOUT THE JOB

- during routine staff meetings
- when informing staff about new job directives issued by senior agency executives
- when informing staff about various changes in work assignments
- when observing staff interact with other supervisors or senior agency executives
- when informing staff about agency policy changes and future agency undertakings
- when staff initiate interactions with the supervisor about job-related events
- when informing staff about significant happenings occurring in the agency that affect other agency staff
- when working side by side with staff

Once supervisors have a good idea about those aspects of the job staff dislike, then supervisors should take active steps to remove or otherwise decrease the occurrence of those aspects. The remainder of this chapter discusses ways in which such steps can be taken. The processes to be presented are based on those features of human service jobs frequently disliked by staff as well as those features over which supervisors can usually exert some control.

Protecting Staff From Being Affected
By Unpleasant Events

Blocking the Jabs

One straightforward means of decreasing bad things in staffs' work environment is to prevent staff from having to experience those things. In particular, a supervisor can prevent staff from being aware certain negative events have taken place. There are activities occurring periodically in any work place that do not have a significant impact on an agency's overall operation, but have a negative impact on staff once staff become aware of the events. We are referring primarily to seemingly insignificant, verbal exchanges occurring with little thought on most people's part but nevertheless detracting from staffs' job enjoyment. These exchanges usually consist of negative statements about a staff person's job performance, statements we refer to as verbal jabs. Jabs represent relatively minor, negative events affecting a staff person in contrast to events having an immediate, crucial impact on a staff person's work enjoyment. Nevertheless, usually when staff hear someone has complained about their performance, staff experience an unpleasant feeling. The negative effect of the verbal jab intensifies if the jab is repeated. Repeated jabs tend to seriously wear away at a staff person's work enjoyment. Hence, an action a supervisor can take to decrease one bad thing in staffs' work environment is to prevent staff from hearing about certain negative comments. We call this process blocking the jabs.

The process of blocking the jabs is perhaps best illustrated by a rather common occurrence among senior executives, and what supervisors can do to decrease the negative outcome of the executives' action for their staff. Many senior executives

— although there are certainly admirable exceptions — do not routinely practice the guidelines stressed earlier of frequently observing staff perform their jobs. Consequently, the executives do not have first hand, objective information about how staff are performing in the work place. The executives tend to respond to second hand information based on what other personnel say about a particular staff person's work behavior.

The people to whom executives listen in the situation just noted are typically agency personnel who spend the most time with the agency executives. The latter people may be administrative assistants or other agency executives, who also do not observe routine staff performance very frequently. Like the senior executives themselves, the people to whom the executives listen do not have objective information regarding staffs' routine performance. The latter individuals will, however, hear about something a staff person has done through the work grapevine and relay the information to a senior executive without checking the accuracy of what they have heard. Quite frequently, what the individuals pass on to the executive has to do with something negative they have heard about a staff person (i.e., individuals do just the opposite of what was recommended in Chapter 6, they say bad things about people behind their backs — even without knowing whether what they are saying is accurate). The senior executive, who also fails to investigate the accuracy of what was said, in turn passes on to the staff person's supervisor negative concerns about the respective staff person.

The situation just described is particularly problematic if the executive has already made up her mind what was heard was accurate, and has already formed a negative impression about the staff person. When the staff member's supervisor hears the information from the executive, the supervisor should know if the information is accurate based on the supervisor's observations of the staff person's work performance. Hence, the supervisor can readily verify or refute the hearsay. The primary concern here though, is if the information is indeed inaccurate and the staff person hears about the executive's negative concerns, the end result is an unwarranted, bad event for the staff person.

The detrimental effect the scenario just described has on a staff person's work enjoyment is well understood if the reader thinks about having experienced such a situation. As alluded to earlier, anyone who hears a senior executive is displeased with him does not have particularly good feelings about the news. The feelings usually are even worse if the individual knows the executive's displeasure is based on inaccurate information passed on to the executive by someone else. The negative feelings one experiences may exist even if the executive is not overly concerned with the situation and only mentioned it to someone else (e.g., the staff person's supervisor) as a passing comment; the staff person really does not know how seriously the executive is concerned, only that she has expressed displeasure.

The first thing a supervisor should do in the situation just described is determine if the information even needs to reach the respective staff person. If the supervisor knows the information about the individual is inaccurate but the staff person is nevertheless likely to be bothered by the executive's expressed displeasure about him, the supervisor simply should not inform the staff person about the situation. The supervisor protects the individual from the effects of the comments — by blocking the (verbal) jabs.

SUPERVISORS SHOULD PROTECT STAFF FROM CERTAIN INACCURATE, NEGATIVE COMMENTS ABOUT THEIR PERFORMANCE

If a staff person never hears about an executive's negative comments, then the comments cannot have a harmful effect on the staff person's work enjoyment. Of course, the supervisor should not let the situation rest without some response to the executive. Once an executive believes something negative about a staff member regardless if the belief is based on accurate information or not, the executive is more likely to believe other negative things about the staff person even if the latter things are inaccurate. The supervisor should first prevent the negative comments from reaching the staff person and then take steps to rectify the inaccurate impression held by the agency executive. The latter steps may involve meeting with the executive and changing her mind by presenting accurate, positive information about the staff person's performance. Alternatively, the supervisor may take steps to ensure the executive directly observes or hears through other people good aspects about the staff person's performance. In short, if the supervisor takes the route of protecting the staff person from hearing about the bad information, then the supervisor should see to it the situation is not likely to happen again.

Collecting the Garbage

The example just provided represents a means by which a supervisor can protect staff from unpleasant events that really should never happen in the first place (i.e., bad events due to rumors). There are also some things that appropriately occur in human service agencies resulting in a demoralizing effect on staff that a supervisor can likewise prevent from affecting staff. What a supervisor can do in the latter situations is "collect the garbage." In this case the garbage refers to miscellaneous duties requiring considerable staff time and effort that do not enhance staffs' performance of their primary duties, and may even detract from their regular duties. Supervisors can prevent staff from experiencing these types of negative work requirements and thereby decrease potentially bad things in staffs' work environment by finding a way to have the duties completed without staff having to complete the tasks themselves.

An illustration of the type of situation just referred to occurs when the head office of a human service agency requires the agency to complete a one-time, but time-consuming, administrative task. For example, the central office of a large operation overseeing group homes for people with developmental disabilities may send each group home manager a directive to provide demographic information on the agency's clients (e.g., number of clients who do not exhibit independent toileting skills, number of clients who engage in challenging behavior on a daily basis). Frequently, by the time the request reaches each group home manager the information is needed immediately, representing an administrative crisis for the manager. A typical response of a group home manager to such a request is to present the task to the direct service staff who know the most about the clients, with a directive to complete the task immediately. Staff then have to find a way to work the task of obtaining and writing/summarizing the information into their existing schedule, requiring extra time and effort for the staff.

While staff may be well aware an administrative task as just referred to needs to be completed, they usually are not particularly thrilled about having to immediately respond to an unexpected administrative requirement. Often such directives are presented to staff in a manner overly stating the significance of getting the task done and getting it done quickly. Staff may not understand or agree with why the request is so important, and may even view the task as much less important than providing the direct service typically occupying their work time. The latter view becomes intensified for staff when they have to forego completing daily responsibilities normally expected of them by agency executives. In short, what is considered a rather crucial task in the central administrative office may not be considered nearly as crucial by direct service staff. The end result is staff become disgruntled about having to complete the seemingly unimportant task with undue urgency.

An alternative strategy in the situation just described for the group home manager to prevent staff from becoming disgruntled is for the manager to find a means of completing the administrative task without involving staff. If the manager can fulfill the task without staff involvement, then there will be no disgruntlement among staff and in essence, one bad thing that can happen in staffs' work environment is prevented from occurring. The most likely means to have the task completed is for the supervisor to complete the task himself; the manager would "collect the garbage" for the staff. Of course, this strategy means the manager can experience the same disgruntlement staff would experience, and particularly if the manager has the same view as staff regarding the relative unimportance of the task. If the manager views completing the task though as one means of enhancing staff work enjoyment by preventing a bad thing from occurring for staff, then the impact of completing the task can make the supervisor feel good because he has done something nice for staff. Completing job duties for staff that staff find unpleasant to perform assists a supervisor in answering the question raised in Chapter 6 of "What have I done to help motivate my staff?" by noting something specific the supervisor has performed to motivate his staff.

SUPERVISORS SHOULD PROTECT STAFF FROM HAVING TO PERFORM UNNECESSARY AND UNPLEASANT TASKS

The number of unpleasant tasks supervisors can complete for staff is of course going to be limited. Supervisors have their own duties to complete. Hence, supervisors need to be aware of other means of "collecting the garbage" for staff. From the perspective of preventing a particular bad thing from happening in staffs' work environment, it does not matter how the supervisor gets the task completed as long as staff do not have to be involved in completing the task. How the supervisor completes the task depends on the supervisor's available resources and creativity. One strategy we have found useful is to know if there is a given staff person who may not mind performing a certain administrative task relative to how most staff would view having to complete the task, and then soliciting that person's assistance. It also helps to ensure a considerable amount of positive feedback is provided to the staff person once she completes the task (Chapter 5).

A second strategy for completing extra administrative tasks for staff is to solicit the help of a secretary if one is available. We have often found secretaries' skills to be under utilized in human service settings. We have worked with many secretaries who enjoy special jobs that differ from their routine duties, and particularly if the secretaries know by assisting the supervisor in completing the task they are helping to avoid disgruntlement among other staff.

Another means of preventing staff from having to complete unpleasant tasks occasionally arising is to employ temporary help. Although this means may be unworkable in some agencies because supervisors lack sufficient control over tem-

porary employment funds or because it is a bureaucratic night-
mare to actually use the funds, in other agencies the process is
not very difficult. Generally, one effective strategy to quickly
employ temporary help is to arrange to have a fund set aside for
such purposes and to have certain individuals on standby for
periodic, part-time assistance. The initial process for establishing a temporary employment fund and securing people willing
to occasionally help may be effortful for a supervisor, but once
the monies and people are arranged the subsequent benefits for
the supervisor (and correspondingly the staff) can be substantial. The important point here is supervisors should reserve at
least some use of the temporary employment funds to complete
periodic tasks for staff that staff do not like to complete themselves.

Sorting Through the Garbage

A means of decreasing negative aspects of staffs' work environment quite similar to collecting the garbage is "sorting
through the garbage." Sorting through the garbage is helpful in
situations in which a supervisor cannot totally prevent staff from
having to perform a particularly unpleasant job duty. When the
supervisor must solicit staff assistance in completing such a task,
the supervisor can make the task less unpleasant for staff by
reducing the amount of time or effort required of staff to complete the task; the garbage is sorted by the supervisor.

Using the example provided earlier involving the group
home manager's response to the administrative directive, the
manager may realize he cannot realistically comply with the
directive without help from the direct service staff. The manager could, however, minimize the extra burden on staff by determining how the task could be streamlined. Streamlining may
involve, for example, preparing forms for the staff to complete

to reduce their time in preparing a written summary of the requested information. Similarly, the supervisor might complete some information on the forms for staff that is standard across all clients or is easily obtainable from client records or other sources. The point is a supervisor should attempt to determine how extra work required of staff can be reduced as much as possible. As with the process of collecting the garbage, the supervisor's goal is to: (1) get the task done and, (2) reduce the negative aspects of the task for staff. When considered in this light, the extra effort required of the supervisor to sort through the garbage can be viewed as active steps taken to make staffs' job less unpleasant — and therefore, create a more motivating work environment for staff.

Distributing the Garbage

Although the strategies of collecting and sorting the garbage are useful means of reducing bad things in staffs' work environment, the strategies are not foolproof. Despite a supervisor's best efforts, there will be times when she must heavily involve staff in completing unpleasant duties separate from staffs' usual day-to-day duties. When the latter situations arise, it can be helpful if the supervisor "distributes the garbage." Distributing the garbage involves rotating the unpleasant duties across staff over time. In brief, each staff person takes a turn completing a "garbage" work task.

Distributing the garbage has several benefits in terms of reducing bad things in staffs' work environment. First, by taking turns, each staff person does not have to be involved in every unpleasant task needing to be completed. Second, staff usually view the process as a fair way to have the tasks completed. No single staff person is likely to feel he is being unfairly picked on because everybody participates over time in performing the unwanted duties. Staffs' view of the process as fair, and therefore at least relatively acceptable, can be further enhanced if the supervisor also participates in taking a turn in completing the tasks (see discussion of supervisors helping out in Chapter 8).

Other Means of Decreasing Bad Things In Staffs' Work Life

Minimizing the Worries

One of the most unpleasant situations for staff in human service agencies, as well as any work setting, is to be in a state of constant or frequent worry. Frequent worrying is accompanied by high levels of anxiety, and anxiety is a most unpleasant feeling, not to mention an unhealthy state. Worrying and anxiety often are the result of knowing, or at least suspecting, something major is going to happen in the work place yet not knowing exactly what will happen nor when it will happen. In short, uncertainty about events in one's work life leads to worry and anxiety. Hence, another bad thing in staffs' work environment a supervisor should strive to eliminate or minimize is staff uncertainty about forthcoming, significant events in the work place. Supervisors should maintain frequent contact with staff and inform staff as quickly as possible when the supervisor becomes aware of changes likely to occur in the work environment. The goal is to accurately and comprehensively inform staff of what may happen before staff hear inaccurate or incomplete information about possible changes through the work rumor mill, and before staff begin to worry about how the changes will affect them.

ONE OF THE MOST UNPLEASANT ASPECTS OF A JOB IS FREQUENT WORRY ABOUT POTENTIAL, UNDESIRABLE CHANGES IN ONE'S WORK LIFE

Events resulting in staff anxiety in human service settings can be quite varied. However, an event almost always resulting in significant anxiety and worry among staff is rumors regarding "Reduction In Force" (RIF) or staff layoffs. Readers who have worked in an agency facing a RIF situation can readily attest to the serious anxiety a RIF generates among an agency's work force. A supervisor can minimize the anxiety by ensuring staff stay well informed about all aspects regarding the RIF and how it will or will not affect them. In order to keep staff well informed, the supervisor must do two general things. First, the supervisor must actively and persistently seek information from appropriate agency personnel who know or are deciding the RIF status. Second, once the supervisor obtains relevant information about the RIF, the supervisor should quickly share the information with staff. Again, the goal is to reduce or prevent anxiety among staff by preventing staff from being uncertain about their future work life.

Hopefully, readers will not have to worry about a RIF situation in their agency in the near future. There are a number of other potential events in human service agencies though that can result in considerable worry and anxiety among staff if staff are uncertain about how the events will affect them. If, for example, staff hear through the work grapevine their agency is going to be opening up new service sites and some staff may be transferred to the new sites, considerable anxiety is likely to develop among staff who have no desire to move to a new location. Other agency events often resulting in worry and anxiety among staff when staff become aware of the events through the rumor mill include changes in work schedules such as different hours assigned to work each day, a change in staffs' supervisor, admission of clients to the agency who have a serious and/or contagious disease, and major changes in work duties. As with the RIF situation noted earlier, the worry such events evoke among staff can be minimized if the supervisor informs staff about the plans before any information regarding the potential changes reaches staff through the rumor mill.

SUPERVISORS CAN REDUCE STAFF WORRY OVER POSSIBLE BAD EVENTS BY ROUTINELY KEEPING STAFF ABREAST OF FORTHCOMING CHANGES IN THE WORK ENVIRONMENT

Although the process of keeping staff abreast of agency plans regarding potential work changes is presented here as a means of decreasing one bad thing (i.e., staff worry due to uncertainty about the job) in staffs' work environment, the process also has the effect of increasing good things. Staff can be quite appreciative of supervisors who regularly take the time to interact with staff to share information about forthcoming agency events. However, it should also be noted it is essentially impossible to always provide staff with information about potential job changes before staff begin to suspect something significant is about to happen. The informal rumor mill in many agencies functions as a well-oiled machine, and staff can become aware of upcoming changes before the staff supervisor has any idea about the events. Supervisors can still reduce staff anxiety in such situations though, by quickly obtaining and sharing accurate information about the potential changes when the supervisor becomes aware something may happen. Often, the supervisor's awareness will initially occur when staff question the supervisor about the changes. At that point the supervisor's job from a motivational standpoint is to quickly find out what is going on and relay the information to staff in a quick, accurate, and hopefully, reassuring manner.

Minimizing Negative Reactions

The preceding chapter section discussed what supervisors can do prior to major changes occurring in staffs' work environment to minimize unpleasant worry and anxiety among staff. Sometimes supervisors can totally prevent or eliminate anxious feelings among staff by determining the suspected changes will never actually occur (in these cases staffs' rumor mill was not accurate). However, there will also be changes occurring from time to time in any human service agency that staff perceive as undesirable and as such, represent bad things in staffs' work environment. The changes hopefully are for the good of the agency's clients overall, even if there is a detrimental effect on staffs' quality of work life. Indeed, supervisors of direct service staff periodically have to make unpleasant changes themselves, such as altering staffs' work schedule due to staff shortages. In other cases senior executives within the agency make changes staff dislike — changes over which staff supervisors have no control. When unpleasant changes do occur within an agency, the supervisor's job from a motivational perspective is to minimize the negative impact of the changes on staff. The following sections describe several strategies supervisors can use to decrease the bad aspects of changes in staffs' work situation on staffs' overall work enjoyment.

Participative Management Strategies. The beneficial effects of participative management strategies for increasing staffs' enjoyment with their work were discussed in Chapter 6. Participative management strategies are also useful for minimizing staffs' negative reactions to undesired changes in the work place.

In particular, it can be most advantageous to involve staff in the planning stages for determining how certain changes will occur. As referred to in Chapter 6, staff are usually more accepting of managerial actions if they are involved in the initial planning of those actions.

In some cases it is not possible to involve staff in the planning for changes in agency operations, and especially when the staffs' supervisor herself is not involved in the planning. However, a participative management approach can still be helpful when informing staff about the planned changes. When supervisors themselves become aware of changes to occur in an agency, the supervisors should take the time to thoroughly inform staff about the changes and most importantly, why the changes are deemed necessary. Most staff are more accepting of unpleasant changes when they know precisely why the changes need to occur relative to if they are simply told about the changes without a good, honest explanation. As presented below, staff also are generally accepting of changes if supervisors follow several guidelines when informing staff about forthcoming changes.

Face-To-Face Strategies. Face-to-face supervisory strategies represent a rather obvious interaction style on the part of supervisors when informing staff of upcoming changes: supervisors inform staff of the changes in a direct, face-to-face manner. Simply put, most staff prefer to be informed of an upcoming change in their work life through a direct interaction with their supervisor, or directly from whomever is responsible for bringing about the change.

The manner in which staff are informed about undesirable changes in work place activities frequently does not involve a face-to-face interaction in a number of human service agencies. For example, we have experienced situations in which staff were informed through a written memorandum their weekly work schedule had unexpectedly been changed to a less desirable schedule, without any explanation or interaction from a supervisor or executive person. We have likewise experienced situations in which staff were informed through a computer E-mail message their client caseload was being significantly increased. Perhaps most noticeably, we have observed staff handed a reprimanding memorandum about their performance by an administrative assistant or other designee instead of being delivered by the person initiating the reprimand. In the latter cases, the staff received no interaction directly from the person who was criticizing their performance.

The situations just exemplified in which face-to-face interactions did not occur are particularly bothersome for staff for two general reasons. First, these methods of informing staff about changes in their work routine do not allow staff the opportunity to ask questions about why the actions are occurring. Without the opportunity to discuss and ask questions, staff cannot become very well informed about the necessity of the changes. As noted earlier, lack of information about why changes are occurring can increase staffs' negative reactions to the changes. Second, and more importantly, staff tend to devalue agency superiors who do not meet personally with staff to inform them of events likely to decrease their overall work enjoyment. Such devaluation tends to increase staffs' negative reactions to the agency changes even further.

Most supervisors with whom we have interacted over the years readily agree with the importance of face-to-face interaction styles with staff. Hence, in one sense it is somewhat surprising face-to-face strategies are not used routinely in many agencies when informing staff about unpleasant changes in their work life. In some cases the agency supervisors or executives making the changes simply do not stop and think about the effect of the changes on staff, and simply want to get the word out about the changes quickly. In other cases, supervisors or executives basically are not concerned about the negative impact of the changes on staff and just want the changes to happen. Relatedly, some individuals know staff are likely to respond to the changes negatively, and those individuals do not want to have to deal with the negative staff reactions themselves.

In order to avoid increasing staffs' negative reactions to unpleasant changes in agency work operations, we strongly advocate face-to-face interaction styles for informing staff about the changes. A good rule of thumb is whoever is responsible for making the changes be the person who meets with staff to inform them of the changes. In agencies employing large numbers of staff such that face-to-face interactions by a senior executive or other person responsible for making the changes is not practical, the face-to-face strategy should be implemented through the agency chain of command. That is, the person responsible for the changes should meet face-to-face with the people who report directly to her to inform them about the changes and allow them the opportunity to ask questions. The latter individuals in turn should meet face-to-face with the people who report directly to them in the chain of command. The same face-to-face process should continue until everybody affected by the agency changes has met with their immediate supervisor for information sharing.

PEOPLE RESPONSIBLE FOR MAKING AGENCY CHANGES THAT STAFF ARE LIKELY TO PERCEIVE AS UNDESIRABLE SHOULD MEET FACE-TO-FACE WITH ALL STAFF AFFECTED BY THE CHANGES

Respect-During-Absence Strategies. The strategies discussed to this point for reducing the negative impact on staff of
certain changes in the work place have focused on interactions
supervisors should have with staff. To reiterate, supervisors
should interact with staff to make sure staff are thoroughly informed why agency changes need to occur. The interactions
should be face-to-face in contrast to using a messenger, memo
or computer message to inform staff. Using such strategies,
supervisors can proactively attempt to reduce the unpleasantness changes in work operations cause for staff. This section
discusses a different strategy related to informing staff about
agency changes that focuses not on what supervisors should
proactively do per se, but what supervisors should avoid doing.

The practice we are referring to that should be avoided by
supervisors pertains to making changes in work operations having a serious impact on staffs' work life while staff are tempo-
rarily absent from work. Of course, depending in part on how
long a respective staff person is away from work, some changes
must occur regardless of a staff person's absence. However,
we have observed changes in agency operations clearly affecting a staff person's work life that were made while the staff
person was absent from work for only a week or so; changes
that easily could have waited until the staff person had returned
to work in order to inform the staff person about the changes in
a face-to-face manner. Agency changes we have observed in
this regard include the alteration of a staff person's work shift
assignment from a more preferred day shift to a less preferred
night shift schedule, re-assignment of part of a staff person's
daily work responsibilities to another staff member and replace-
ment of the former duties with less desirable assignments, and
in the most extreme example, actually laying off staff while
staff were on vacation leave from work.

Making changes in work operations affecting a staff person's work life without the staff member's awareness while he is absent from work can have a devastating effect on the staff person's work enjoyment. Any reader who has returned from a short vacation or sick leave and unexpectedly found his office had been moved, some of his staff had been re-assigned to another supervisor, his travel budget had been expended by another department, etc., can readily attest to the negative impact the changes have on one's work enjoyment. Actually, it is probably surprising to some readers these types of actions are carried out by human service executives — the actions represent quite unadmirable work behavior. However, other readers can undoubtedly provide a number of other examples of similar types of actions they have observed in human service agencies. Changes in work operations occur in various agencies while staff are absent for essentially the same reasons provided earlier regarding why some executives do not engage in face-to-face interactions about agency changes.

The reason the actions just illustrated are so detrimental for staffs' work enjoyment and subsequent work motivation is two-fold. First, by their nature these actions are unexpected by staff; staff typically do not expect to take approved leave from work and then return to work to find their job has been significantly altered in an undesirable manner. Once staff undergo an unexpected change while away from work, the staff develop serious uncertainty about the stability of their daily work routine. Staff begin to feel if major changes in their job can occur without any forewarning, and when they are not even around, basically any number of unexpected events could occur with their job. The uncertainty leads to worry and anxiety which, as discussed earlier, represent a very bad thing in staffs' work environment.

The second reason changes in work operations while staff are absent from work are typically so devastating is the actions cause staff to devalue the agency superiors who are responsible for the changes. Staff lose respect for the superiors because the manner in which the superiors implement the changes seems underhanded to the staff. The loss of respect has a long-standing impact on staffs' enjoyment in the work place because the less respect staff have for a given superior or boss, the less staff enjoy working for that person. The detrimental impact that disrespect for an agency superior can have on one's work enjoyment can be readily understood by those readers who have worked for a number of different executives over the years. For whom have the readers enjoyed working more, the superiors they respected or the superiors they did not respect? Our interactions with supervisors consistently have indicated most people enjoy their jobs more when they work for someone they respect.

Chapter 8

THE SUPERVISOR AS A MOTIVATOR

Preceding chapters have presented actions supervisors can take to motivate their staff by increasing the amount of enjoyment staff experience in the work place. If supervisors consistently implement the procedures described to this point, a typical outcome is staff not only enjoy what the supervisors do for the staff, but staff also come to enjoy the supervisors themselves. Staff will enjoy working for the supervisors overall and, simply enjoy the supervisors' presence. When supervisors are viewed by staff in this light, then the supervisors themselves can function as a positive motivator for staff. As such, the supervisors represent one more good thing existing in staffs' work environment.

SUPERVISORS THEMSELVES CAN REPRESENT A GOOD THING IN STAFFS' WORK ENVIRONMENT

The desirable effect supervisors can have on staffs' work enjoyment when the supervisors themselves function as a motivator is perhaps best exemplified by considering two common situations in human service agencies and the resulting impact on staff. One situation pertains to the practice of monitoring staff performance. As discussed in preceding chapters, monitoring is an important function of a supervisor for ensuring proficient staff performance. As also discussed previously though, most staff do not particularly like having their performance monitored — at least in regard to how monitoring typically occurs in human service agencies. To illustrate, readers should consider the typical reactions they have had when a supervisor unexpectedly entered their work space to monitor their work performance. Our experience suggests the initial feeling readers will recall is not an especially pleasant one. Rather, many people experience apprehension, anxiety, or outright fear when their supervisor comes to monitor their performance. In such situations, supervisors usually are not functioning as a motivator themselves, or at least not as a positive motivator. If however, supervisors follow the procedures discussed in preceding chapters, as well as in this chapter, the latter situation can be turned around such that staff actually like it when their supervisor enters their work place for monitoring purposes.

WHEN A SUPERVISOR FUNCTIONS AS A POSITIVE MOTIVATOR, STAFF ACTUALLY LIKE TO HAVE THE SUPERVISOR COME TO THE STAFFS' WORK PLACE

A second situation exemplifying whether or not a supervisor functions as a positive motivator pertains to certain types of interactions a supervisor initiates with staff. Readers are asked to envision the situation in which they receive a message informing them their supervisor must meet with them the very first thing the next morning. Again, our experience suggests the initial reaction among a number of readers upon hearing their supervisor has called an impromptu, "must-attend" meeting is one of some apprehension — perhaps a feeling something is wrong and the meeting means bad news for the reader. Alternatively, if the supervisor has established herself as a positive motivator, the initial reaction will not be a negative one but a positive or even excited feeling. When a supervisor is a positive motivator for staff, staff typically look forward to interactions with the supervisor.

As indicated in the situations just described, a supervisor herself can have a rather profound effect on a staff person's work enjoyment. For purposes of motivation as defined throughout this text, it is most beneficial if the effect is an enjoyable one for staff. When a supervisor is successful at establishing herself as a positive motivator, two desirable outcomes result from an overall motivational perspective. First, bad things in staffs' work environment, as exemplified by negative feelings staff experience in the situations just illustrated, are decreased. Second, the opposite, or pleasant, experiences resulting from the situations just noted represent good things that are increased in staffs' work environment.

The process of a supervisor functioning as a positive motivator herself does not happen overnight. The process takes time — time during which staff repeatedly associate the supervisor with good things happening in the staffs' work environment. When staff consistently observe a supervisor being responsible for, or otherwise being associated with, good things happening in their work life, staff develop respect and trust for their supervisor. Staff respect the supervisor for what the supervisor does to help the staff, and trust the supervisor has a sincere interest in staffs' quality of work life. This chapter discusses several specific things supervisors can do to enhance the likelihood the supervisors themselves will function as a positive motivator for staff. As indicated earlier, the strategies to be discussed should be considered in addition to the positive motivational strategies already described in preceding chapters.

Strategies For Helping Supervisors
Function As Positive Motivators For Staff

Helping Out

When staff express things they like about their supervisor, one of the most consistently reported likes is the supervisor is willing to "help out"—the supervisor will periodically join staff during their routine work situation and help staff complete their duties. Staff are usually very appreciative of supervisors who are willing to do the same job tasks staff have to do on a day-to-day basis. Hence, one important thing a supervisor can do to increase the likelihood staff will like the supervisor, and therefore help the supervisor become a positive motivator himself, is to demonstrate the willingness to help staff perform their duties.

In order for supervisors to increase their motivational value among staff by helping out, supervisors must of course have the skills to perform the tasks their staff are expected to perform. In most situations pertaining to direct service staff in the human services, supervisors typically do have the work skills to help staff perform their primary job duties. As noted in Chapter 3, many supervisors of direct service staff were promoted to the role of supervisor from the ranks of direct service because of exemplary direct service performance themselves. In those less frequent cases, however, where supervisors have not acquired direct service work skills, it is recommended supervisors readily acknowledge their work-skill shortcomings and quickly strive to acquire the skills by working with their staff. Supervisors who cannot proficiently perform the same duties expected of their paraprofessional, direct service staff usually have many more problems motivating their staff relative to supervisors who have direct service work skills in their performance repertoire.

Although the process of a supervisor helping out can significantly enhance the supervisor's role as a positive motivator, there is a caution to heed when considering the process. Specifically, there is a point of diminishing returns with how much time is spent helping out. Supervisors have their own jobs to perform and should not spend so much time helping out that the latter efforts interfere with their own job duties. There is no hard and fast rule for exactly how much time supervisors should spend helping out. Typically though, it is recommended at least some time each week be spent helping out.

SUPERVISORS SHOULD SPEND AT LEAST SOME TIME EACH WEEK HELPING OUT WITH THEIR STAFF

Stand-Up Supervising

Helping out as just described represents something a supervisor can do on a relatively frequent basis to enhance how much staff like the supervisor, and consequently increase the supervisor's value as a positive motivator himself. A process in which supervisors can participate on a less frequent basis, but nevertheless representing something staff usually like about a supervisor, is when the supervisor "stands up" for staff. Standing up for staff is similar in many ways to collecting the garbage (preventing staff from having to perform unpleasant, extra work duties) and blocking the jabs (preventing staff from coming into contact with, or hearing about, events that would affect staff unpleasantly) discussed in Chapter 7. However, stand-up supervising is presented as a separate supervisory strategy here because it typically has more of an impact on staffs' positive perception of the supervisor relative to the former procedures.

A supervisor stands up for staff by making serious, overt attempts to stop senior executives or managers from taking actions affecting staffs' work life in a manner staff seriously dislike. There are a variety of situations in human service agencies in which it can be beneficial for supervisors to stand up for their staff and attempt to change an executive decision that would adversely affect staff. One example pertaining to most types of human service settings involves the client caseload with whom a respective group of staff work on a day-to-day basis. Whenever a given client caseload is changed by an executive decision such as by adding new clients to the caseload, the staffs' work life is going to be affected. Often, the change in client caseload is made without any input from the direct service staff and by executives who have no first hand knowledge regarding the amount of staff duties associated with staffs' existing caseload. Supervisors of direct service staff need to have a good idea if staff have a full caseload and whether staff can realistically take on additional clients. If an executive decision is being considered to increase a caseload that is already full, and especially if the increase involves expecting staff to provide services to a client with difficult needs such as severe behavior problems, a supervisor can stand up for staff by convincing the executive not to increase the caseload.

In the situation just described, increasing the client caseload would result in unrealistic and perhaps impossible work responsibilities for staff, as well as less than optimal services for the client who is being added to the caseload. Hence, the supervisor should strive to stop the executive action by, for example, convincing the executive the client should be served elsewhere, or services should be withheld until there is realistic room within the staffs' caseload. In short, the supervisor should stand up for staff by preventing the executive from putting an unmanageable work load on staff.

As readers are likely to conclude from the preceding example, although stand-up supervising can be a powerful means for a supervisor to acquire positive motivating qualities with staff, this supervisory strategy can be a difficult task for supervisors. The difficulty is due to several issues supervisors must resolve if stand-up supervising is to be successful. First, by the nature of human service organizations, like any work operation, senior executives have the designated authority and responsibility to make decisions regarding agency functioning, even if the decisions can detrimentally affect staffs' work life. The senior executives (who, in this case are represented by anyone higher in the organizational management structure than the supervisor) also have more authority in this regard than the supervisor. When the supervisor is convinced an executive's decision will have a negative effect on staff and stands up for his staff by attempting to prevent the executive's actions, the supervisor is in the vulnerable position of overtly disagreeing with one of his superiors. Such actions by the supervisor can result in negative or retaliatory responses by the executive and have a detrimental effect on the quality of the supervisor's work life.

A second issue related to stand-up supervising is sometimes executive decisions are made in the best interest of the agency's clients even though the impact on staffs' work life is quite unpleasant. Supervisors have to make the difficult decision regarding whether the beneficial impact of executive actions on client welfare outweighs the negative impact on staff motivation. If the effect on staff motivation is too detrimental, the actions may actually harm client welfare. As emphasized in

Chapter 1, when staff are poorly motivated, client welfare inevitably suffers.

A third issue with stand-up supervising is supervisors have to decide if the performance of staff whose work life will be detrimentally affected by an executive decision represents performance for which the supervisor should stand up and support. If a supervisor defends staffs' position on an executive decision when staff are not performing proficiently, and the executive is aware staff are not doing a good job, the executive's view of the supervisor's judgement is not likely to be a particularly admirable view. If the latter process is repeated very often by the supervisor, the executive will begin to seriously devalue the supervisor's judgement overall. Consequently, it will be much more difficult for the supervisor to effectively stand up for staff when indeed staffs' job performance warrants standing up for — because the executive will not put much credence in the supervisor's opinion. Relatedly, if supervisors routinely stand up for staff regardless of staffs' performance, supervisors run the risk of being viewed as agency personnel who value staff welfare at the expense of client welfare. In short, supervisors should stand up for their staff only in those situations in which staffs' performance clearly warrants support by the supervisor.

When considering stand-up supervision, and especially in light of the potential difficulties with the process as just noted, a complex situation that can arise is when the supervisor knows she will not be able to change an executive decision regardless of the negative impact on staff. In one sense, stand-up supervision in this case may seem to be a practice in futility. In another sense though, and especially for staff motivational purposes, there are benefits of supervisors sometimes standing up for staff even when the supervisors know they cannot change the executive's decision. Staff can be very appreciative of their supervisor if they are aware the supervisor has sincerely tried to affect the executive's decision-making. Staff usually know when the supervisor attempts to prevent something bad from happening in the staffs' work life by overtly disagreeing with her boss, the supervisor can run some serious job risks. As a result, staff simply knowing the supervisor stood up and tried to support the staff can help the staff view the supervisor in a good light — a light that helps the supervisor become a positive motivator herself.

STAND-UP SUPERVISING CAN BE RISKY FOR SUPERVISORS BUT BENEFICIAL FOR STAFF

Cover-Up Supervising

Cover-up supervising as a means of assisting a supervisor to acquire motivating qualities himself is similar in several ways to stand-up supervising. As with stand-up supervising, the purpose of cover-up supervisory procedures is to prevent a bad thing from happening in staffs' work environment. As also with stand-up supervising, cover-up strategies focus on a potential bad thing for staff resulting from a particular type of senior executive action. However, as discussed in the following paragraphs, there are some noticeable differences in these two motivational approaches, even though both strategies help a supervisor establish himself as a positive motivator for staff.

Cover-up supervising is a means by which a supervisor can provide support for a respective staff person who typically performs her duties in a satisfactory manner, but during an isolated incident engages in obviously inappropriate work behavior. Any staff person, no matter how well skilled and motivated, is going to make some mistakes in the work place from time to time. Cover-up supervising is a means by which a su-

pervisor can prevent the staff person from receiving highly negative consequences for the occasional mistake; consequences that
can have a detrimental impact on the staff person's work motivation.

The most likely type of seriously negative consequence for
a staff person's isolated performance problem stems from a senior executive's overreaction to the problem. The executive may
hear about the staff person's undesirable work activity through
someone besides the staff person's immediate supervisor, such
as an administrative assistant. The executive then demands
immediate and rather severe punitive action for the staff person. The action is mandated without the executive evaluating
whether the problematic performance represents typical work
behavior on the part of the staff person. As presented here, the
staff member's problem performance is indeed an isolated incident and clearly dissimilar to the staff person's usual satisfactory performance. Hence, the staff person's performance really
should not be severely punished because the problematic work
incident is an unusual event and as such, is not likely to happen
again. When a performance problem is not likely to be repeated,
there is no reason to provide a severely negative consequence
for the problem. As discussed in Chapter 5, due to detrimental
effects of seriously negative consequences on staff motivation,
such consequences should only be provided when they are necessary to decrease the likelihood of certain behaviors from occurring in the future.

When the type of situation just described occurs, a supervisor should of course provide corrective feedback to the staff
member (again, see Chapter 5) so the staff person knows what
she did is wrong, and is informed about how she could handle
the incident more appropriately in the future. Actually, in this
type of case, which involves a staff person who usually per-

forms without mistakes, the staff person typically is well aware of her mistake at work and does not need much corrective feedback. More importantly, the staff person certainly does not need severe punitive action. However, because the executive has no first hand information the incident is noncharacteristic of the staff person's performance and not likely to be repeated, the executive believes the staff person should be seriously punished.

When an executive mandates significant punitive actions for a staff person that the supervisor believes are unwarranted, a supervisor can prevent the actions from detrimentally affecting the staff person through cover-up supervision. The supervisor can cover for the staff person by informing the executive the staff person should not be severely punished because she was operating under the supervisor's direction. The supervisor covers for the staff person by convincing the executive the problematic incident was in essence, the supervisor's fault and not the fault of the staff person. Most executives will not follow through with punitive action when the supervisor convinces the executive the supervisor was more at fault than the staff person.

Covering up for a staff member as just described represents a supervisory strategy many staff seriously appreciate on the part of their supervisor. As such, cover-up supervising helps the supervisor become more highly valued by staff. In turn, the process assists the supervisor in acquiring motivating qualties himself among the staff.

As many readers have undoubtedly concluded at this point, cover-up supervision can represent a risky strategy on the part of the supervisor. The supervisor essentially is informing an agency executive the supervisor himself has performed in a poor manner, or at least is responsible for his staff performing in a poor manner. All the risk factors described earlier with stand-up supervision pertain to cover-up supervision. Consequently, the same guidelines discussed with stand-up supervision should be followed regarding the use of cover-up supervisory strategies. To reiterate briefly, cover-up supervision should occur infrequently on the part of a supervisor. Actually, if other supervisory strategies discussed in this book are adhered to, and especially the strategies presented in Chapters 3 - 5, cover-up supervision will not be needed often because staff will not make many performance mistakes that catch the attention of agency executives. A second guideline for using cover-up supervision is the process should occur only when staffs' performance is routinely satisfactory or above satisfactory such that their performance warrants the supervisor covering for them.

COVER-UP SUPERVISING SHOULD OCCUR ONLY FOR THOSE STAFF WHOSE OVERALL PERFORMANCE WARRANTS STRONG SUPPORT BY A SUPERVISOR

Cover-up supervision has been discussed to this point as a means of enhancing the motivational quality of a supervisor himself. There are some occasions though in which cover-up supervision really does not enhance a supervisor's motivational value for staff per se, but nevertheless is still important from a motivational perspective. Specifically, there are some staff who do not want their supervisor to cover for their performance deficiencies. These staff are aware the supervisor can place himself in a precarious position with an agency executive by covering for the staff, and they do not want to put the supervisor in such a position (note: in such situations the supervisor usually is already functioning as a motivator himself for staff as the staff have a high degree of respect for the supervisor). Other staff simply feel responsible for their actions and believe they should suffer the consequences for their own work behavior, even if the consequences could have a rather devastating effect on their quality of work life.

Consequences provided for isolated performance problems can be devastating for staff because the staff are aware the executive is providing negative consequences at a degree of severity that is unwarranted based on the performance incident. Similarly, this type of executive action makes the staff person very aware: (a) the executive does not know the staff person typically performs well in the work place and, (b) the executive has not bothered, when becoming aware of the work problem, to investigate the situation to learn the incident is highly unusual relative to the staff person's typical performance. Both of the latter two factors cause a staff person to devalue the agency executive and can be most demoralizing to a hard working staff person, with a harmful effect on the staff person's work motivation.

In light of the detrimental effects of the executive's actions on the staff person's quality of work life, a supervisor can cover for staff even if the supervisor believes staff may not want the supervisor to necessarily cover for them for reasons just noted. In this type of case, the supervisor simply covers for staff without informing the staff. The staff remain unaware of the intended executive action and simply receive the appropriate, corrective feedback from the supervisor as described earlier. The supervisor convinces the executive the supervisor was primarily the person at fault in contrast to the staff and everybody gets back to business as usual.

Because the supervisor's cover-up actions in the situation just described are unknown to staff, the actions cannot serve to enhance the motivational qualities of the supervisor himself. However, the cover-up strategy still serves to stop a bad thing from happening in staffs' work environment by preventing the punitive actions the staff would receive. As such, the cover-up action plays an important role in enhancing the motivational qualities of staffs' work environment overall. As discussed in Chapters 6 and 7, providing a motivating work environment for staff entails increasing good things and decreasing bad things in staffs' work environment; preventing a needless punitive action from occurring represents one means of prohibiting a bad thing from happening to staff.

A Final Comment on The Effects of Supervisors Establishing Themselves as A Motivator

Throughout this chapter, as well as preceding chapters, the focus has been on positive motivating strategies for supervisors to conduct with their staff. Positive strategies are stressed because they serve the dual purpose of assisting staff in working hard and enhancing staffs' enjoyment with their work. However, as every reader is undoubtedly aware, there are times when supervisors must take negative actions with staff. As described in Chapter 5, from an OBM perspective negative actions are sometimes necessary when staff perform in an inadequate manner regarding designated work expectations. Using an OBM approach, supervisors must inform staff the performance was not adequate as well as how the performance should occur in the future. There are also other times when highly serious performance problems occur and more punitive sanctions must be implemented, such as formal disciplinary action, to decrease the likelihood a staff person will engage in the problem behavior again.

When supervisory actions are taken as just noted, no matter how positively the supervisor attempts to implement the procedures staff will experience the actions with a certain degree of unpleasantness. In short, corrective or punitive supervisory actions rarely have any enjoyment value for staff. The actions can, however, assist staff in improving their work performance by working more diligently and/or more proficiently. As such, the actions play an important role from time to time in a supervisor's job of motivating her staff.

When a supervisor must provide corrective feedback or more serious punitive actions with staff, the effectiveness of the supervisory procedures is enhanced immeasurably if the supervisor has established herself as a positive motivator for staff. In essence, the more positive motivating qualities a supervisor has with staff, the more effectively the supervisor will be able to use negative consequences to help staff improve their work performance. The impact of a supervisor's positive motivating qualities on the effectiveness of negative consequence procedures is twofold. First, and most importantly, when the positive procedures presented throughout this book for helping staff work hard and enjoy their work are routinely used by a supervisor, there will be infrequent need for corrective and punitive actions with staff. Staff will be performing quite effectively most of the time and seriously inadequate work performances will be rare.

SUPERVISORS WHO HAVE ESTABLISHED THEMSELVES AS A POSITIVE MOTIVATOR FOR STAFF RARELY HAVE TO TAKE SERIOUS PUNITIVE ACTION WITH STAFF

The second impact, which is related to the infrequency of need for negative supervisory actions, involves a contrast effect with the use of negative actions. Because staff are accustomed to their supervisor using positive strategies, when the supervisor implements negative procedures to correct performance problems the procedures stand in stark contrast to the supervisor's usual actions. By standing out as something noticeably different on the part of the supervisor, the negative actions evoke serious attention among staff. The heightened attention staff give to the supervisor's negative actions cause the actions to have a more powerful effect on staffs' performance relative to if staff are used to receiving negative actions.

The contrast effect just described allows a supervisor who is routinely positive with staff to affect changes in problematic staff performance with relatively minor negative consequences. If staff are use to a supervisor praising appropriate work performance, for example, one simple negative comment from the supervisor can have a major effect on staff performance. To illustrate, if a routinely positive supervisor points out how a staff person is not completing a work assignment as quickly as she should, the comment can have a profound impact on the staff person's attempts to complete the assignment more efficiently. The criticism by the supervisor draws serious attention from the staff person because she is not use to receiving critical comments from the supervisor. Also, the staff person is usually impressed by the seriousness of the supervisor's concern with her work performance because the criticism represents a rare and unusual action by the supervisor; an action staff typically conclude would not be taken unless the supervisor was seriously concerned.

Contrary to the example just provided, if a staff person is use to receiving negative actions from a supervisor, a simple comment by the supervisor about not completing work efficiently represents a rather routine occurrence for the staff person. As such, the staff person has no reason to give any extra attention to the supervisor's comment because the staff person hears those types of comments seemingly all the time. In order for a supervisor to have a significant impact on the staff person in the latter situation, the supervisor would have to take much more punitive action than usual, such as suspension from work or threat of dismissal.

In summary, if a supervisor is routinely positive with staff, the supervisor does not have to use highly punitive actions to change staffs' inadequate work performance. Minor negative procedures will be sufficiently effective when negative actions are needed. Minor negative actions by a supervisor have much less of a detrimental impact on staffs' quality of work life relative to severe negative actions and therefore, contribute more beneficially to creating a motivating work environment.

Chapter 9

MOTIVATING THE MOTIVATORS: SELF-MOTIVATION FOR SUPERVISORS

Throughout this text we have focused on active steps supervisors can take to motivate their staff. We have repeatedly asserted a routine part of a supervisor's day-to-day job is to do specific things to ensure staff are working hard and enjoying their work. The more frequently a supervisor can answer the question raised in Chapter 6 of "What have I done to help my staff work hard and enjoy their work?" by referring to specific actions the supervisor has completed, the more likely the supervisor's staff will be working in a highly motivating environment. When considering the various actions supervisors must take in this regard, it becomes clear the staff motivational requirement of a supervisor's job can entail a significant amount of time and effort. In order for supervisors to perform their staff motivational duties successfully, the supervisors themselves must be well motivated. This chapter discusses means through which supervisors can ensure they are indeed well motivated to perform their duties.

IF SUPERVISORS ARE TO EFFECTIVELY HELP THEIR STAFF WORK HARD AND ENJOY THEIR WORK, THE SUPERVISORS THEMSELVES MUST BE MOTIVATED TO WORK HARD AND ENJOY WHAT THEY DO IN THE WORK PLACE

Senior Executives as Motivational Sources for Supervisors

In light of the important role a supervisor plays in motivating his direct service staff, it logically follows whoever supervises the staff supervisor in the organizational chain of command can play a significant role in motivating the supervisor. Senior personnel in human service agencies who have management authority over supervisors of direct service staff possess both the means and the responsibility to ensure their supervisory personnel are working in a motivating environment. As undoubtedly a number of readers have experienced, many executives in human service agencies are quite effective at providing a positive, motivating work environment for their direct service supervisors. However, as a number of readers are also likely aware, there are many other executive personnel who do not provide a pleasant or motivating work environment for their staff supervisors.

Exactly why some senior agency personnel effectively motivate their staff supervisors and why some do not represents a book's worth of dialogue in its own right. In most cases though, there are two basic reasons for executive inadequacy in providing a motivating environment for supervisors of direct service staff. First, some senior executives simply do not have the "know how" to motivate their staff supervisors. Second, some executives simply are not very concerned with the motivational welfare of staff supervisors.

Lack of "know how" in respect to motivating supervisors is due essentially to inadequate work skills among senior personnel. To illustrate, in many cases senior personnel did not earn their way into upper eschelon jobs within the agency due to exemplary work skills. Rather, the executives obtained their jobs because they had certain personal or political ties to high-ranking agency administrators. The lack of motivational know how among the executives often relates in turn to lack of significant concern for motivating staff supervisors. When senior executives do not have the skills to perform their jobs effectively, they not only do not know how to motivate the people whom they supervise (i.e., the staff supervisors), they really do not have time to be concerned with the welfare of the people whom they supervise. The executives must spend inordinate amounts of time trying to impress their bosses in order to defend and protect their status in the organization. These individuals also can be seriously threatened by the competence of the staff supervisors who report to them — supervisors who actually have better work skills than the executives. The executives are not especially interested in helping the supervisors work diligently and enjoy their work because the better the supervisors perform their jobs, the more threatening the staff supervisors are to the executives.

The preceding examples present some of the worse case scenarios regarding executives who are responsible for overseeing work performance of staff supervisors but do not provide a motivating environment for the supervisors. As indicated previously, there are many senior agency personnel who perform in just the opposite manner and represent valuable sources of motivation for staff supervisors. We present the negative examples here, however, to make the point supervisors should not assume their bosses will necessarily be concerned with providing a positive and motivating work environment for the supervisors. If staff supervisors are fortunate to indeed work for effective motivators, the supervisors should be grateful and actively strive to support the desirable work practices of their executives. Even in such situations though, staff supervisors should be prepared for the time when they do not work for competent executives. Our experience suggests there will be times when most staff supervisors will work in a situation in which they cannot rely on their boss to motivate them. In the latter case, as well as those situations in which supervisors are already working in a setting without an adequately skilled executive, the supervisors must find alternative sources of motivation. Supervisors must find motivational sources over which they can exert control themselves.

The best source of motivational inspiration over which supervisors can always have significant control is the motivation staff supervisors specifically provide for themselves. In short, supervisors must be skilled in self-motivation. Just as with the focus in previous chapters on supervisors taking active steps to assist their staff in working hard and enjoying their work, supervisors must be able and willing to take active steps to motivate themselves.

SUPERVISORS SHOULD NOT ASSUME THEIR BOSSES WILL EFFECTIVELY MOTIVATE THEM; SUPERVISORS MUST ACTIVELY TAKE STEPS TO MOTIVATE THEMSELVES

Self-Motivation For Supervisors

There are a variety of strategies supervisors can use to acquire and maintain the motivation to work hard themselves and enjoy their work. The primary point is supervisors cannot be expected to effectively increase work effort among their staff if the supervisors themselves are not putting forth consistently diligent work effort. Supervisors likewise cannot be expected to effectively enhance the work enjoyment of their staff if the supervisors do not enjoy at least a large portion of their own work. Actually, when supervisors are successful in motivating themselves, that fact alone will help motivate their staff. When staff frequently observe their supervisor working hard while overtly enjoying what she is doing, the work effort and enjoyment tends to rub off on staff; staff themselves will acquire some of the same work characteristics they observe with their supervisor.

Goal Setting

The importance of establishing goals for enhancing job performance among human service personnel has been discussed in preceding chapters. To briefly reiterate, it can be helpful to have work goals to direct work efforts, and subsequently to have the opportunity to experience the satisfaction of achieving a desired goal. Work goals can also have a significant self-motivational benefit for supervisors.

Work goals for supervisors can be considered as falling within two general categories: long-term and short-term. Long-term goals refer to major accomplishments to strive for in the work place that typically take a considerable period of time to accomplish, usually months or years. These are the types of goals previously referred to with staff that set the occasion for staff experiencing a high level of job satisfaction with accomplishing something very worthwhile as part of the job — satisfaction that has a significant motivational effect. In terms of supervisor motivation, the impact of having clearly established, long-term goals to strive to achieve is twofold, and in accordance with the essence of motivation. First, when a supervisor establishes a job goal he thinks would be important to obtain, the existence of the goal in the supervisor's mind can cause the supervisor to work more diligently (to obtain the goal) relative to if there is not a long-term goal to function as a work incentive. Second, when a supervisor actually fulfills a major work undertaking, the resulting personal and professional satisfaction derived from achieving the goal can be a significant source of enjoyment in the work place. Fulfilling an important goal can make the supervisor feel quite good about his work accomplishment, and feeling good about work enhances the supervisor's work enjoyment.

Although long-term goals can have a significant effect on the work motivation of supervisors in human service agencies, by their nature such goals have limitations. In particular, the work enjoyment derived from achieving a long-term goal is not going to occur very often. Long-term goals requiring a year or two to accomplish, for example, will result in work enjoyment only every other year or so. Because of the inherent infrequency with which work enjoyment results from achieving long-term goals, we place more importance on the second type of goal in regard to self-motivation for supervisors. Specifically, short-term goals typically have a more frequent and pervasive impact on a supervisor's self-motivation.

Short-term goals pertain to specific objectives supervisors establish and strive to obtain on a daily or weekly basis. These goals involve much smaller time and effort investments on the part of supervisors relative to long-term goals. For example, a long-term goal for a supervisor may be to establish a privately operated incentive fund to use to reward staff monetarily or to employ temporary help to complete particular work tasks for staff (see Chapter 7 for discussion of using part-time help to relieve staff of periodic, unpleasant duties). To achieve such a goal, a supervisor may have to meet with many people to obtain approval for the fund, establish banking procedures, determine and implement means of generating start-up monies, etc. Such procedures typically require at least a few months to complete.

In contrast, a short-term goal to be achieved within a given work week may be as simple as completing an appropriate orientation procedure for a new employee. A short-term goal to complete within a respective work day may be to meet with a seemingly disgruntled staff person to determine what is bothering the staff member.

As the examples just noted reflect, there are many types of short-term goals supervisors can establish in the work place. In essence, anything a supervisor believes is important to perform as part of her day-to-day work operation can be established as a goal for the day or week. Although the significance of setting these types of goals may not be readily apparent at first glance — because fulfillment of the goals represents in large part what supervisors should be doing as part of their routinely assigned duties — establishing goals to achieve on a daily or weekly basis can nevertheless help a supervisor ensure she becomes and stays highly motivated.

Short-term goals can affect supervisors' self-motivation in three basic ways. First, the establishment of work goals helps direct supervisors' work efforts because the goals make it clear to supervisors what they want to accomplish on a day-to-day basis. As such, short-term goals can enhance supervisors' work diligence relative to the rather common situation in which supervisors find themselves simply doing the same duties every day without the realization they are ever finishing anything. In the latter situation supervisors merely "put in their time" and basically feel they do the same thing every day without ever reducing their work load, similar to what can happen to direct service staff as described in Chapter 6. In contrast, once a supervisor establishes a daily work goal, the supervisor has something to strive for every day because there is a clear work objective to complete.

A second impact of short-term work goals is when the goals are met by the end of the work day or week, supervisors can experience a certain degree of satisfaction for having accomplished something. As noted already, satisfaction from completing and reaching closure on a work duty represents one source of work enjoyment. Relatedly, by establishing and achieving short-term goals, supervisors set the occasion to actively reinforce themselves for a job well done. The act of supervisors reinforcing their own fulfillment of a work goal is the third beneficial outcome of short-term goals. When supervisors can frequently reinforce themselves for their successful work accomplishments, they are in effect taking charge of their own work motivation.

SELF-REINFORCEMENT ALLOWS SUPERVISORS TO TAKE CHARGE OF THEIR OWN MOTIVATION

Self-Reinforcement By Supervisors

The process of supervisors reinforcing the performance of their staff as a means of increasing staffs' work effort as well as work enjoyment was highlighted in Chapter 5. Supervisors can use the same basic process to reinforce their own performance and correspondingly, enhance their work motivation. Supervisory self-reinforcement as a means of increasing work performance and enjoyment involves the following general procedures. Initially, as described in the previous chapter section, the supervisor must establish a short-term work goal to achieve by the end of the work day or week. Again, any work responsibility the supervisor views as important can represent a short-term goal. It also can be helpful from a motivational standpoint if the work duty is not only important, but something the supervisor does not especially like to perform. The latter duties are those job tasks supervisors tend to delay performing until the last possible minute, or avoid doing altogether. Most readers can probably think of duties important to complete, but duties the readers dread actually performing. For many supervisors, these duties are represented by laborious administrative tasks such as completing various work reports for their boss, making new work schedules for their staff for the upcoming month, completing summaries of unusual incidents such as staff or client injuries, etc. By targeting those relatively less desirable but necessary tasks for self-reinforcement processes, supervisors not only increase the likelihood they will complete the tasks in a timely manner, but also make completion of the tasks more enjoyable than usual.

The second step in the supervisory self-reinforcement process is an obvious one, that of actually completing the task. We only mention this step here to emphasize the importance of supervisors using self-reinforcement based on their work accomplishments. As with reinforcing staff performance, self-reinforcement is effective from a self-motivational standpoint only if the reinforcement is dependent on supervisors completing important work duties.

The final step in the self-reinforcement process involves a supervisor doing something enjoyable for herself when she achieves the designated work goal — the supervisor provides her own positive consequence following her desirable performance. What a respective supervisor specifically does to reinforce her work performance depends on the supervisor's own work situation and individual preferences. Hence, the types of self-reinforcers to use in the work place are highly varied across different supervisors and human service agencies.

There are several useful guidelines for assisting supervisors in determining how to reinforce their work performance.

One rather apparent guideline is whatever a supervisor does to reinforce her completion of job duties should be an acceptable work activity in accordance with agency policy. Using an activity as a reinforcer for successfully achieving a work goal that is disallowed or frowned upon by agency executives is going to place a supervisor in a precarious situation with her superiors.

The second general guideline for selecting self-reinforcers can facilitate a supervisor's adherence to the first guideline of choosing reinforcing activities that are acceptable within the supervisor's agency. Specifically, a supervisor can use regular work activities she enjoys performing as reinforcers for fulfilling work responsibilities she does not like to perform. When arranging the work routine in this manner, the supervisor is not doing anything as part of self-reinforcement that is likely to be viewed as unacceptable by agency executives because the supervisor's time spent reinforcing herself involves performing job-related duties.

The primary point in the self-reinforcement process just exemplified is the supervisor withholds engaging in a more preferred work activity until she has successfully completed a less preferred duty. To illustrate, upon completion of a less desirable administrative task as discussed earlier, the supervisor may deliberately spend time participating with a favorite client in an enjoyable leisure activity — an activity both the supervisor and client enjoy doing. Alternatively, if a supervisor enjoys working with certain staff because the staff are productive and pleasant, following completion of a less desirable task the supervisor may schedule time to work with the respective staff on a task the staff and supervisor view as important and enjoyable.

SUPERVISORS CAN REINFORCE THEIR OWN WORK PERFORMANCE BY PURPOSEFULLY ENGAGING IN AN ENJOYABLE WORK ACTIVITY FOLLOWING SUCCESSFUL COMPLETION OF A LESS DESIRABLE WORK DUTY

Another guideline for selecting a means of self-reinforcing obtainment of a work goal is to arrange something to do after work hours to reinforce work performance. We frequently have a special dinner or night out with our spouse or family when we achieve an important goal at work. This process does not appeal to everyone though, because some people prefer to totally separate their work life from their family or nonwork life. However, taking some aspect of work home in the form of doing something desirable after work typically has minimal if any bad effects related to what people usually think of when mixing work and nonwork activities. Reinforcing one's own work performance through an enjoyable, after work activity represents a self-motivational means of taking home the goods referred to in Chapter 6. In this case, in contrast to motivating staff by helping staff take home the goods, the supervisor is helping to motivate herself by arranging reinforcing events after work.

SUPERVISOR SELF-REINFORCEMENT INVOLVES ESTABLISHING A WORK GOAL, ACHIEVING THE GOAL, AND THEN DOING SOMETHING ENJOYABLE

Self-Managing The Bad

The self-motivational strategies for supervisors discussed to this point pertain essentially to ways of increasing good things in the supervisor's work life. In summary, by establishing goals and self-reinforcing achievement of those goals, supervisors can increase their work effort as well as the amount of enjoyment they experience in the day-to-day work routine. Such a process allows a supervisor to be in control of his own work motivation, which in turn helps a supervisor be in control of his own quality of work life. Another important component of self-motivation for supervisors pertains not to increasing the good things in the work place, but decreasing or at least coping with the bad things. As with any job, supervisory positions in the human services are going to involve unpleasant situations from time to time. To maintain a high level of motivation, every supervisor must effectively manage undersirable situations that can demoralize or otherwise interfere with a supervisor's motivation to perform his job.

Although the types of situations detrimentally impacting a supervisor's work motivation are many and varied, there is one particular situation that typically affects supervisory motivation most seriously. We are referring to situations in which a supervisor and his staff are performing their duties at a satisfactory level yet something highly unpleasant happens that is for all intents and purposes, quite unwarranted. These are situations in which the supervisor is doing a nice job, or at least is doing as well as can be realistically expected given the resources and environment in which the supervisor works, and unexpectedly receives a major negative consequence for his work. In short, the supervisor's good work efforts and the good work efforts of his staff are seriously punished. Presented below are some scenarios supervisors have experienced in human service agencies reflecting these types of situations; situations that can be most devastating to a supervisor's work motivation.

Scenario 1: A supervisor turns in the name of a staff member to be promoted to a higher level position in the agency based on exemplary performance of the staff member and a senior executive negates the promotion recommendation by promoting an employee who has a poor performance record but has a special social, familial or political relationship with the executive.

Scenario 2: A supervisor and his staff work diligently and effectively to improve an area of client service provision and that area is subsequently severely criticized by an external evaluation team or governmental regulatory body based on an incomplete or otherwise inaccurate evaluation of the service provision.

Scenario 3: A supervisor waits for extended periods of time to allow his staff to receive deserved pay raises and when money becomes available for staff raises, it is redirected to give a hefty pay raise to a select group of executive or administrative personnel instead of the staff.

Any reader who has experienced one or more of the scenarios just illustrated can attest quite readily to the negative impact such actions have on a supervisor's work motivation. Of course, in some cases there may be reasonable explanations why the actions occur. In the first scenario, for example, the executive who overrides the supervisor's promotion recommendation may have more valid information regarding qualifications of the person the executive promoted relative to the supervisor's nominee for promotion. However, even when there are some justifiable reasons for the actions illustrated in the scenarios, the supervisor may not be made aware of the reasons. In other cases, there simply are no valid reasons, or the seemingly justifiable reasons are really a dishonest guise to hide the real reasons. Regardless, one major outcome of these types of situations is a supervisor's motivation to work diligently, much less to strive to enhance the work effort and enjoyment of his staff, is seriously impeded.

When supervisors experience the types of situations just exemplified, they must take active steps to manage the "bad" events in order to prohibit the situations from seriously hurting their self-motivation. Where possible, supervisors should naturally try to stop the actions from actually coming to fruition. As noted earlier though, some bad things, no matter how unwarranted, are going to happen from time to time. In order to effectively maintain work motivation and manage the unavoidable bad things that do occur, there are two general strategies supervisors can employ: setting limits to the bad and overcoming the bad with the good.

MAINTAINING SELF-MOTIVATION INVOLVES EFFECTIVELY DEALING WITH UNWARRANTED BAD THINGS HAPPENING IN A SUPERVISOR'S WORK ENVIRONMENT

Setting Limits to the Bad. The first step in the limit-setting process entails a supervisor determining what negative events can realistically happen in the work place that are of significant importance to him. There are numerous events in any human service agency having an unpleasant effect on a supervisor yet when the supervisor thinks about the events in a truly objective manner, he realizes the events are not very important and do not warrant serious concern. When viewed in an objective manner, a supervisor can easily determine no matter how unpleasant or unjustified some events are, the events do not have an important effect on the supervisor's ability to adequately perform his job.

To illustrate the type of situation just referred to, readers should think back over the last several years and identify events that at the time seriously bothered them, but currently each reader realizes the distress experienced was basically needless. Most readers will recall such events and can be somewhat amused at how rather insignificant occurrences had such an unnecessary but nevertheless stressful effect on them. To prevent this type of reaction from occurring in the future, a supervisor can set limits to the types of events that he will allow to upset him. Generally, there are not many events worth becoming seriously upset about in the long run. If a supervisor determines those events that bothered him in the past but upon retrospective analysis the events had no serious or lasting effect on anything important in the work place, then the supervisor can consciously decide not to let those things bother him in the future.

Another illustration of the type of situation we have been referring to is an employee who "talks the talk" but does not "walk the talk". Most readers can identify someone with whom they have worked who talked a most impressive game to a top agency executive—so impressive the executive considered the employee an outstanding asset to the agency and constantly praised the employee publicly. Impressing the top agency executive by in essence, saying things the executive wants to hear, is not necessarily wrong and can actually be a good job survival skill (assuming of course whatever is said is honest; individual ethics should not be compromised just to please a boss with impressive talk). However, the problem arises, and what tends to bother supervisors, when the employee does not "walk the talk". The employee talks a good game for the boss but does not perform well at all in terms of completing job duties at a satisfactory level. It can be most bothersome to a supervisor when an executive frequently praises someone who talks a good game but, perhaps unknowingly to the executive, performs her job much less effectively than the supervisor's staff. The supervisor's reaction becomes more disconcerting when the supervisor's staff perform their jobs more admirably than the employee who receives the executive's commendation but the former staff receive much less, if any, commendation from the executive.

The scenario just described should not occur in human service agencies. The executive is doing good things for an employee who, in terms of providing agency services, does not deserve praiseworthy commendation and particularly when compared to the lack of commendation for staff who perform their duties more proficiently. However, the world of work is by no means perfect and such situations do arise. The important point for supervisory motivation is supervisors should not let this type of inappropriate activity by the agency executive and his "pet" employee bother the supervisor. When a supervisor seriously thinks about what is important in his own work life, it does not matter very much what a respective executive does with another employee. What is important is what the executive does with the supervisor and the supervisor's staff. The supervisor should focus on his performance and interactions with the executive and simply ignore the executive's erroneous interactions with the employee who earns her keep through talk and not performance.

Using the type of situation just noted as an example, it is helpful for supervisors to list all the work events that seriously bother them. Subsequently, supervisors should identify which of those events really are not important in the long run and as such, are not worth causing the supervisors to become upset. Supervisors should then consciously determine they are not going to be bothered by those particular things in the future.

These steps allow supervisors to set limits as to how many things are going to cause them to become upset at work. The more things supervisors can determine they are not going to be bothered by, the greater the reduction in bad things in supervisors' work environments. Correspondingly, as bad things in the work place are reduced, the quality of supervisory work life is improved.

Although the limit setting process can be beneficial for decreasing bad things in supervisors' job routines, realistically the process is often easier said than done. Many of us become upset about things when we know we should not; we simply are not always able to control our emotions even though we know the emotions are unwarranted and unpleasant. To enhance a supervisor's ability to set limits and not be bothered by basically insignificant events in the work place, it can be helpful for a supervisor to periodically verbalize the limit setting process to others. Specifically, as bothersome events occur, a supervisor should first evaluate the significance of the events. Next, if upon objective scrutiny the events appear too unimportant to warrant becoming upset, the supervisor should share this observation with staff, other supervisors, etc. Explaining to others that even though an unpleasant event is uncalled for, the event will not have any significant job impact and does not warrant worrying about has a nice self-control component for the supervisor: the process reminds the supervisor not to become upset himself.

Another, related outcome of the limit setting process is it allows a supervisor to obtain a certain peace of mind by preventing the supervisor from worrying about things that might happen later in the work place. As discussed in Chapter 7, worrying has a very negative effect on staff work enjoyment, and worrying has the same detrimental impact on supervisors. By eliminating worry over events that could occur in the work place in the future, another bad thing in supervisory work life is prevented from happening.

For many supervisors, the worst type of possible event causing frequent or periodic worry and anxiety is the thought of losing one's job due to being fired, reductions-in-force, layoffs, etc. Many supervisors cannot ever totally remove the fear of losing their jobs, and particularly in current times when many corporate and human service enterprises are adopting the staff down-sizing philosophy as a means of reducing the cost of their operations. Anxiety over job loss can plague a supervisor periodically for years on end, representing a serious obstacle to maintaining high levels of work motivation.

In all honesty, we cannot offer suggestions totally guaranteed to stop supervisors from ever worrying about their job security. The best advice we can offer when supervisors find themselves frequently experiencing anxiety over possible job loss is to: (a) think through all the consequences of losing the current job and, (b) determine how to deal with each of those consequences. Often, when a supervisor thoroughly envisions all consequences realistically as well as the strategies for handling the consequences, she finds that job loss, even as the potentially worst thing to happen in the work place, is not as devastating as it appears at first glance. It can also be helpful for a supervisor to simply determine that in many cases, job loss will be something over which she has no control. As such, there is no reason to worry about potential job loss. In short, there is absolutely no benefit in worrying about something one cannot control.

ALL SUPERVISORS SHOULD REALIZE THERE IS NO BENEFIT IN WORRYING ABOUT SOMETHING THEY CANNOT CONTROL

In addition to threat of job loss, there can be a number of other events supervisors view as being among the worst things possibly happening in the work place that can be dealt with using the limit setting process. Related to the down-sizing scenario just noted, it may be a supervisor is aware agency executives are considering transferring one of the supervisor's key staff persons to another work site, or laying off the staff person altogether. Further, the executives are considering the action without any input from the staff person's immediate supervisor. Such a possibility may be extremely worrisome to the supervisor because, for example, the supervisor knows the event would be most devastating to the employee. What can make matters worse is when the supervisor knows quite well the employee contributes more to the welfare of the agency's clients than other agency staff whose jobs are not in potential jeopardy.

In the situation just illustrated, the supervisor is aware an executive is considering an action based either on inaccurate information or even worse, inappropriate motivation. The action may result from inaccurate information because the executive mistakenly determines who is providing the better client services and subsequently terminates the more satisfactory worker. Alternatively, the action may be inappropriately motivated because the executive retains an unsatisfactory worker due to social or political ties the staff member has with the executive, and terminates the more satisfactory worker who does not have such ties. Regardless, the supervisor is aware that for the wrong reasons, a good employee can experience a devastating situation. The thought of such an event can bother a supervisor enormously. The supervisor knows the action will hurt a staff member whose performance actually warrants reward and not job loss. Also, the reason for the decision can infuriate the supervisor and seriously conflict with the supervisor's professional ethics.

Although the type of inappropriate job action just illustrated represents a situation we and others have observed, such activity does not occur in every human service agency. What actually represents the worst types of events to potentially occur in each supervisor's work place is dependent on what is of most importance to respective supervisors, as well as the idosyncratic events occurring in different human service agencies. Our concern here is supervisors must find a way to manage the worry and anxiety resulting from the thought of such actions occurring, whatever they may be, in order to prevent the supervisor's work motivation from being seriously hampered.

In order to effectively manage anxiety and related unpleasant emotions accompanying concern over bad things that could happen in the work place, supervisors can set limits as to what they will put up with as part of their jobs. Of course, supervisors should first do whatever is reasonable to prevent the events from occurring in the first place. At times though, there will be some things despite a supervisor's best preventive efforts that the supervisor is still not totally convinced will not happen. To manage anxiety associated with the latter situations, a supervisor should seriously think about and subsequently determine what type of unethical, unprofessional or otherwise unacceptable things could happen in the agency that would go beyond the supervisor's level of tolerance. A supervisor can then determine what type of event is so intolerable that if it does indeed occur, the supervisor will resign her position within the agency to maintain her ethics and self-respect. In short, supervisors should consciously set limits to what they will put up with on the job.

Once a supervisor determines events that may occur in her agency resulting in cause for her to resign, a significant amount of the worry a supervisor experiences over such events possibly occurring typically will be greatly diminished. As such, the supervisor is gaining a degree of control over the anxiety associated with having to experience extremely unpleasant events in the job. The supervisor is taking control of her work destiny by determining the conditions under which she will and will not work for a respective agency and its executives. When a supervisor truly reaches closure in this manner, the supervisor comes to grips with the realization that if the worst thing that could happen to the supervisor does indeed happen, the supervisor knows she can handle it.

Overcoming the Bad With the Good. The limit setting process just described is one of the best ways for a supervisor to avoid frequent feelings of minor displeasure as well as serious discontent due to potential, or actual, negative events in the work place. However, as alluded to earlier, we by no means intend to imply the limit setting process is fool-proof. Even when a supervisor is extremely successful at limit setting, things will happen in the supervisor's agency that can really bother the supervisor. In the latter situations, the limit setting process has not worked successfully and the supervisor experiences unpleasant feelings and emotions that seriously interfere with the supervisor's work enjoyment. Additionally, when a supervisor is seriously bothered by an event in the work place, the accompanying emotional reactions the supervisor experiences, whether due to anger, disappointment, or general disillusionment, make it difficult for the supervisor to work diligently. A supervisor's energies become engulfed by her emotional reactions and the energies cannot be directed to performing routine supervisory duties. Consequently, when such situations arise, a supervisor must find a way to manage the negative emotional responses.

One of the best ways to handle the types of situations just noted is to quickly and actively replace negative emotional reactions to bad events with more positive responses. In turn, the best way to replace unpleasant emotional responses is to actively participate in positive work activities generating pleasant emotional responses — responses incompatible with the negative reactions. One simple yet effective means for a supervisor to replace an unpleasant emotional response is for the supervisor to immediately, and repeatedly if necessary, do something nice for a staff person who is doing a commendable job. In Chapter 6 the process of catching staff doing a nice job and doing something nice for staff was presented as a means of helping staff experience an enjoyable work environment. The same process can help supervisors overcome their discontent with events in the work place.

The process of doing something nice for a staff person has several beneficial effects for helping a supervisor overcome negative emotional responses to something bad in the work place. First, when a supervisor does something nice for staff, even as simple as praising a staff person's work performance, the supervisor's negative feelings decrease or go away altogether. It is impossible for a supervisor to continue feeling displeased or angry, for example, while the supervisor is sincerely doing something nice for a staff person; the feelings generated within the supervisor while being nice to someone are simply incompatible with unpleasant feelings. Therefore, the more good things the supervisor does, the less capability the supervisor has for experiencing unpleasant emotions.

The second benefit for a supervisor of doing nice things for staff when a supervisor is attempting to overcome a bad state of mind is the supervisor becomes active. The supervisor has to actively search and find staff doing good things in the work place and then interact with the staff to praise their work. Performing such activities requires the supervisor's attention on something besides whatever is bothering the supervisor. While the supervisor is attending to respective work duties, in this case actively attempting to help staff work hard and enjoy their work by praising commendable staff performance, the supervisor will not be thinking about and hence, be bothered about, bad things in the supervisor's own work life. The longer the supervisor stays active and directs her attention away from the job event that bothered her, the less the event will upset the supervisor when she later thinks about the situation. In short, when a supervisor does good things for her staff, she is also doing good things for her own quality of work life.

Chapter 10

THE DO'S AND DON'TS OF STAFF MOTIVATION—A SUMMARY

Preceding chapters have discussed a wide array of supervisory strategies for motivating human service staff. The focus has been on active steps supervisors can take to ensure their staff work hard and enjoy what they do in the work place. To a lesser degree, the chapters have also discussed supervisory strategies to avoid; strategies that result in an unpleasant and nonproductive work environment. This chapter summarizes the strategies discussed in previous chapters by providing a brief set of motivational guidelines for supervisors.

The following guidelines are presented as supervisory do's and don'ts. The format consists of first presenting the "don'ts" — what supervisors should avoid doing from a motivational perspective. The supervisory "don'ts" are based on common mistakes and misassumptions supervisors make concerning staff motivation during the day-to-day job. Following each supervisory don't is what supervisors should do in the respective situation. The latter practices, the "do's", are based on what OBM research and successful supervisory experiences have indicated to be effective means of motivating direct service staff in human service agencies.

If the following "don'ts" are avoided by supervisors and the "do's" are routinely practiced, supervisors will be well on their way to ensuring their staff work in a highly motivating environment. However, the brief listing of "do's" and "don'ts" should not be taken to mean that staff motivation is an easy task. As noted throughout this text, effectively and positively motivating staff is a never ending process. If supervisors are to be successful in motivating their staff, supervisors must actively work every day on motivational processes. Nevertheless, it can be helpful to have guidelines to periodically remind supervisors of what to do and not do in the work place. The following "do's" and "don'ts" represent such guidelines. The guidelines should be referred to after having read the preceding chapters. Additionally, to assist in adhering to the guidelines, accompanying each guideline is a reference to the chapter in which the guideline is discussed in more detail.

The Do's and Don'ts of Staff Motivation

1. DON'T assume staff are naturally motivated to work hard every day. DO take active steps daily and weekly to positively motivate staff. (Chapter 2)

2. DON'T be complacent with staff who are currently highly motivated. DO build on staffs' existing motivation — take routine steps to ensure highly motivated staff stay highly motivated. (Chapter 6)

3. DON'T expect staff to automatically know what to do on the job. DO specify staff responsibilities as observable and measurable work behaviors. (Chapter 3)

4. DON'T secretly or covertly monitor staff work performance. DO inform staff specifically what aspect of work performance is being monitored, why it is being monitored and how it is being monitored. (Chapter 3)

5. DON'T immediately leave the work site after monitoring staff work performance. DO give feedback to staff about their work performance immediately after monitoring. (Chapter 3)

6. DON'T rely heavily on staff training to resolve staff performance problems. DO follow training with consistent on-the-job monitoring and feedback to resolve staff performance problems. (Chapter 5)

7. DON'T rely on classroom-based instructions, lectures, computers, or videotapes for training new work skills to staff. DO train new work skills through instructions, demonstration, practice, and feedback. (Chapter 4)

8. DON'T rely exclusively on nonsupervisory personnel to train new work skills to staff. DO involve supervisors in some aspect of staff training, and especially the on-the-job training aspects. (Chapter 4)

9. DON'T give special awards or recognition based on social, political, or familial reasons. DO give awards and recognition based on specified and publicized work accomplishments. (Chapter 6)

10. DON'T say bad things about staff behind their backs. DO say good things about staffs' work performance behind their backs. (Chapter 6).

11. DON'T expect pay raises to improve daily job performance. DO use feedback every day to improve and maintain job performance. (Chapter 6)

12. DON'T send messengers, memos or computer messages to deliver bad news to staff. DO inform staff of bad news in a face-to-face interaction. (Chapter 7)

13. DON'T allow major changes in staffs' job routine to occur while staff are absent from work. DO wait until staff return to work to make important job changes. (Chapter 7)

14. DON'T expect staff to consistently work hard and enjoy their work if their supervisor is not working hard and enjoying her work. DO take active steps to motivate yourself as a supervisor. (Chapter 9)

15. DON'T be passive when other agency personnel attempt to assign extra work duties to staff. DO actively protect staff from extra job duties. (Chapter 8)

16. DON'T be passive when staff receive negative consequences from senior agency executives. DO stand up for staff when their performance warrants support. (Chapter 8)

17. DON'T rely on others to provide your motivation as a supervisor. DO take active steps to motivate yourself; take charge of your own work effort and enjoyment. (Chapter 9)

18. DON'T let personal or social feelings affect how you interact with staff at work. DO interact and provide feedback based on job performance. (Chapter 6)

19. DON'T respond to second-hand reports about problems with staff performance. DO investigate performance incidents and respond based on observed indices of work. (Chapter 7)

20. DON'T worry about saying too many positive things about staffs' work performance. DO provide positive feedback for satisfactory work performance as much as possible. (all Chapters)

SELECTED READINGS

The readings referenced on this and the following pages provide supplemental information for topics covered in Chapters 1 - 9. Many of the readings describe the research upon which much of the content of the preceding chapters is based. Other readings provide additional examples of the points made in various chapters. To facilitate selection of those readings most relevant to particular topics of interest for readers, readings are grouped according to the following content areas: (a) specifying and monitoring staff performance responsibilities, (b) training new work skills to staff, (c) feedback and related consequence procedures for changing on-the-job staff performance, (d) participative management strategies, (e) determining acceptable management strategies and, (f) general descriptions of Organizational Behavior Management procedures for improving on-the-job staff performance. It should also be noted though, a number of the readings present information pertaining to several different areas of staff motivation.

Specifying and Monitoring Staff Performance Responsibilities

Alavosius, M.P., & Sulzer-Azaroff, B. (1986). The effects of performance feedback on the safety of client lifting and transfer. *Journal of Applied Behavior Analysis, 23*, 151-162.

Christian, W.P., Norris, M.B., Anderson, S.R., & Blew, P.A. (1983). Improving the record-keeping performance of direct service personnel. *Journal of Mental Health Administration, 11*, 4-7.

Dancer, D.D., Braukmann, C.J., Schumaker, J.B., Kirigin, K.A., Willner, A.G., & Wolf, M.M. (1978). The training and validation of behavior observation and description skills. *Behavior Modification, 2*, 113-133.

Durand, V.M. (1983). Behavioral ecology of a staff incentive program: Effects on absenteeism and resident disruptive behavior. *Behavior Modification, 7*, 165-181.

Egan, P., Luce, S.C., & Hall, R.V. (1988). Use of a concurrent treatment design to analyze the effects of a peer review system in a residential setting. *Behavior Modification, 12*, 35-56.

Epstein, L.H., & Wolff, E. (1978). A multiple baseline analysis of implementing components of the problem-oriented medical record. *Behavior Therapy, 9*, 85-88.

Fitzgerald, J.R., Reid, D.H., Schepis, M.M., Faw, G.D., Welty, P.A., & Pyfer, L.M. (1984). A rapid training procedure for teaching manual sign language skills to multidisciplinary institutional staff. *Applied Research in Mental Retardation, 5*, 451-469.

Fleming, R., & Sulzer-Azaroff, B. (1992). Reciprocal peer management: Improving staff instruction in a vocational training program. *Journal of Applied Behavior Analysis, 25*, 611-620.

Fox, C.J., & Sulzer-Azaroff, B. (1989). The effectiveness of two different sources of feedback on staff teaching of fire evacuation skills. *Journal of Organizational Behavior Management, 10*(2), 19-35.

Goncalves, S.J., Iwata, B.A., & Chiang, S.J. (1983). Assessment and training of supervisors' evaluative feedback to their staff in an operant learning program for handicapped children. *Education and Treatment of Children, 6,* 11-20.

Green, C.W., Canipe, V.C., Way, P.J., & Reid, D.H. (1986). Improving the functional utility and effectiveness of classroom services for students with profound multiple handicaps. *The Journal of The Association for Persons with Severe Handicaps, 11,* 162-170.

Greene, B.F., Willis, B.S., Levy, R., & Bailey, J.S. (1978). Measuring client gains from staff -implemented programs. *Journal of Applied Behavior Analysis, 11,* 395-412.

Gross, A.M., & Ekstrand, M. (1983). Increasing and maintaining rates of teacher praise: A study using public posting and feedback fading. *Behavior Modification, 7,* 126-135.

Horner, R.H., Thompsen, L.S., & Storey, K. (1990). Effects of case manager feedback on the quality of individual habilitation plan objectives. *Mental Retardation, 28,* 227-231.

Jones, H.H., Morris, E.K., & Barnard, J.D. (1986). Increasing staff completion of civil commitment forms through instructions and graphed group performance feedback. *Journal of Organizational Behavior Management, 7(3/4), 29- 43.*

Lattimore, J., Stephens, T.E., Favell, J.E., & Risley, T.R. (1984). Increasing direct care staff compliance to individualized physical therapy body positioning prescriptions: Prescriptive checklists. *Mental Retardation, 22,* 79-84.

Lovett, S.B., Bosmajian, C.P., Frederiksen, L.W., & Elder, J.P. (1983). Monitoring professional service delivery: An organizational level intervention. *Behavior Therapy, 14,* 170-177.

Page, T.J., Christian, J.G., Iwata, B.A., Reid, D.H., Crow, R.E., & Dorsey, M.F. (1981). Evaluating and training interdisciplinary teams in writing IPP goals and objectives. *Mental Retardation, 19,* 25-27.

Parsons, M.B., Cash, V.B., & Reid, D.H. (1989). Improving residential treatment services: Implementation and norm-referenced evaluation of a comprehensive management system. *Journal of Applied Behavior Analysis, 22,* 143-156.

Shoemaker, J., & Reid, D.H. (1980). Decreasing chronic absenteeism among institutional staff: Effects of a low-cost attendance program. *Journal of Organizational Behavior Management, 2(4),* 317-328.

Thompson, T.J., Thornhill, C.A., Realon, R.E., & Ervin, K.M. (1991). Improving accuracy in documentation of restrictive interventions by direct-care personnel. *Mental Retardation, 29,* 201-205.

van den Pol, R.A., Reid, D.H., & Fuqua, R.W. (1983). Peer training of safety-related skills to institutional staff: Benefits for trainers and trainees. *Journal of Applied Behavior Analysis, 16,* 139-156.

Training New Work Skills to Staff

Adams, G.L., Tallon, R.J., & Rimell, P. (1980). A comparison of lecture versus role-playing in the training of the use of positive reinforcement. *Journal of Organizational Behavior Management, 2* (3), 205-212.

Burch, M.R., Reiss, M.L., & Bailey, J.S. (1987). A competency-based "hands-on" training package for direct care staff. *Journal of The Association for Persons with Severe Handicaps, 12*, 67-71.

Delameter, A.M., Connors, C.K., & Wells, K.C. (1984). A comparison of staff training procedures: Behavioral applications in the child psychiatric inpatient setting. *Behavior Modification, 8*, 39-58.

Demchak, M.A. (1987). A review of behavioral staff training in special education settings. *Education and Training in Mental Retardation, 22*, 205-217.

Demchak, M.A., & Browder, D.M. (1990). An evaluation of the pyramid model of staff training in group homes for adults with severe handicaps. *Education and Training in Mental Retardation, 25*, 150-163.

Fabry, P.L., & Reid, D.H. (1978). Teaching foster grandparents to train severely handicapped persons. *Journal of Applied Behavior Analysis, 11*, 111-123.

Farmer, R., Wolery, M., Gast, D.L., & Page, J.L. (1988). Individual staff training to increase the frequency of data collection in an integrated preschool program. *Education and Treatment of Children, 11*, 127-142.

Green, C.W., & Reid, D.H. (1994). A comprehensive evaluation of a train-the-trainers model for training education staff to assemble adaptive switches. *Journal of Mental and Physical Disabilities, 6*, 219-238.

Hundert, J. (1982). Training teachers in generalized writing of behavior modification programs for multihandicapped deaf children. *Journal of Applied Behavior Analysis, 15*, 111-122.

Hundert, J., & Hopkins, B. (1992). Training supervisors in a collaborative team approach to promote peer interaction of children with disabilities in integrated preschools. *Journal of Applied Behavior Analysis, 25*, 385-400.

Jones, F.H., & Eimers, R.C. (1975). Role playing to train elementary techers to use a classroom management "skill package'. *Journal of Applied Behavior Analysis, 8*, 421-433.

Jones, F.H., Fremouw, W., & Carples, S. (1977). Pyramid training of elementary school teachers to use a classroom management "skill package". *Journal of Applied Behavior Analysis, 10*, 239-253.

MacDuff, G.S., Krantz, P.J., MacDuff, M.A., & McClannahan, L.E. (1988). Providing incidental teaching for autistic children: A rapid training procedure for therapists. *Education and Treatment of Children, 11*, 205-217.

Maloney, D.M., Phillips, E.L., Fixsen, D.L., & Wolf, M.M. (1975). Training techniques for staff in group homes for juvenile defenders: An analysis. *Criminal Justice and Behavior, 2*, 195-215.

O'Reilly, M.F., Renzaglia, A., Hutchins, M., Koterba-Buss, L., Clayton, M., Halle, J.W., & Izen, C. (1992).

Teaching systematic instruction competencies to special education student teachers: An applied behavioral supervision model. *Journal of The Association for Persons with Severe Handicaps, 17*, 104-111.

Parsons, M.B., Reid, D.H., & Green, C.W. (1993). Preparing direct service staff to teach people with severe disabilities: A comprehensive evaluation of an effective and acceptable training program. *Behavioral Residential Treatment, 8*, 163-186.

Reid, D.H., & Green, C.W. (1990). Staff training. In J.L. Matson (Ed.), *Handbook of behavior modification with the mentally retarded (2nd edition)* (pp. 71-90). New York: Plenum Press.

Schepis, M.M., & Reid, D.H. (1994). Training direct service staff in congregate settings to interact with people with severe disabilities: A quick, effective and acceptable training program. *Behavioral Interventions: Theory & Practice in Residential & Community-Based Clinical Programs, 9*, 13-26.

Schwartz, I.S., Anderson, S.R., & Halle, J.W. (1989). Training teachers to use naturalistic time delay: Effects on teacher behavior and on the language use of students. *The Journal of The Association for the Severely Handicapped, 14*, 48-57.

Smith, T., Parker, T., Taubman, M., & Lovaas, O.I. (1992). Transfer of staff training from workshops to group homes: A failure to generalize across settings. *Research in Developmental Disabilities, 13*, 57-71.

Stein, T.J. (1975). Some ethical considerations of short-term workshops in the principles and methods of behavior modification. *Journal of Applied Behavior Analysis, 8,* 113-115.

Tynan, W.D., & Gengo, V. (1992). Staff training in a pediatric rehabilitation hospital: Development of behavioral engineers. *Journal of Developmental and Physical Disabilities, 4,* 299-306.

Willner, A.G., Braukmann, C.J., Kirigin, K.A., Fixsen, D.L. Phillips, E.L., & Wolf, M.M. (1977). The training and validation of youth-preferred social behaviors of child-care personnel. *Journal of Applied Behavior Analysis, 10,* 219-230.

Feedback and Related Consequence Procedures for Changing On-The-Job Staff Performance

Alavosius, M.P., & Sulzer-Azaroff, B. (1990). Acquisition and maintenance of health-care routines as a function of feedback density. *Journal of Applied Behavior Analysis, 23,* 151-162.

Azrin, N.H., & Pye, G.E. (1989). Staff management by behavioral contracting. *Behavioral Residential Treatment, 4,* 89-98.

Brown, K.M., Willis, B.S., & Reid, D.H. (1981). Differential effects of supervisor verbal feedback and feedback plus approval on institutional staff performance. *Journal of Organizational Behavior Management, 3*(1), 57-68.

Brown, N., & Redmon, W.K. (1989). The effects of a group reinforcement contingency on staff use of unscheduled sick leave. *Journal of Organizational Behavior Management, 10*(2), 3-17.

Calpin, J.P., Edelstein, B., & Redmon, W.K. (1988). Performance feedback and goal setting to improve mental health center staff productivity. *Journal of Organizational Behavior Management, 9*(2), 35-58.

Durand, V.M. (1983). Behavioral ecology of a staff incentive program: Effects on absenteeism and resident disruptive behavior. *Behavior Modification, 7,* 165-181.

Feldstein, S., & Feldstein, J.H. (1990). Positive reinforcement for submission of timely reports by professional staff in a residential facility. *Education and Training in Mental Retardation, 25,* 188-192.

Ford, J.E. (1984). A comparison of three feedback procedures for improving teaching skills. *Journal of Organizational Behavior Management, 6*(1), 65-77.

Hall, R.V., Panyan, M., Rabon, D., & Broden, M. (1968). Instructing beginning teachers in reinforcement procedures which improve classroom control. *Journal of Applied Behavior Analysis, 1,* 315-322.

Harchik, A.E., Sherman, J.A., Sheldon, J.B., & Strouse, M.C. (1992). Ongoing consultation as a method of improving performance of staff members in a group home. *Journal of Applied Behavior Analysis, 25,* 599-610.

Hawkins, A.M., Burgio, L.D., Langford, A., & Engel, B.T. (1992). The effects of verbal and written feedback on staff compliance with assigned prompted voiding in a nursing home. *Journal of Organizational Behavior Management, 13*(1), 137-150.

Hollander, M.A., & Plutchik, R. (1972). A reinforcement program for psychiatric attendants. *Journal of Behavior Therapy & Experimental Psychiatry, 3*, 297-300.

Hutchison, J.M., Jarman, P.H., & Bailey, J.S. (1980). Public posting with a habilitation team: Effects on attendance and performance. *Behavior Modification, 4*, 57-70.

Iwata, B.A., Bailey, J.S., Brown, K.M., Foshee, T.J., & Alpern, M. (1976). A performance-based lottery to improve residential care and training by institutional staff. *Journal of Applied Behavior Analysis, 9*, 417-431.

Kreitner, R., Reif, W.E., & Morris, M. (1987). Measuring the impact of feedback on the performance of mental health technicians. *Journal of Organizational Behavior Mangement, 1*, 105-109.

Leach, D.J., & Dolan, N.K. (1985). Helping teachers increase student academic engagement rate: The evaluation of a minimal feedback procedure. *Behavior Modification, 9*, 55-71.

McMorrow, M.J., Sheeley, R., Levinson, M., Maedke, J., Treworgy, S., Tripp, T., Casey, M., & Hunter, R. (1991). The use of publicly-posted performance feedback in an inpatient psychiatric treatment setting. *Behavioral Residential Treatment, 6*, 165-181.

Panyan, M., Boozer, H., & Morris, N. (1970). Feedback to attendants as a reinforcer for applying operant techniques. *Journal of Applied Behavior Analysis, 3*, 1-4.

Parsons, M.B., Schepis, M.M., Reid, D.H., McCarn, J.E., & Green, C.W. (1987). Expanding the impact of behavioral staff management: A large-scale, long-term application in schools serving severely handicapped students. *Journal of Applied Behavior Analysis, 20*, 139-150.

Patterson, E.T., Griffin, J.C., & Panyan, M.C. (1976). Incentive maintenance of self-help skill training programs for nonprofessional personnel. *Journal of Behavior Therapy & Experimental Psychiatry, 7*, 249-253.

Patterson, R., Cooke, C., & Liberman, R.P. (1972). Reinforcing the reinforcers: A method of supplying feedback to nursing personnel. *Behavior Therapy, 3*, 444-446.

Pomerleau, O.F., Bobrove, P.H., & Smith, R.H. (1973). Rewarding psychiatric aides for the behavioral improvement of assigned patients. *Journal of Applied Behavior Analysis, 6*, 383-390.

Quilitch, H.R. (1975). A comparison of three staff-management procedures. *Journal of Applied Behavior Analysis, 8*, 59-66.

Quilitch, H.R. (1978). Using a simple feedback procedure to reinforce the submission of written suggestions by mental health employees. *Journal of Organizational Behavior Management, 1*(2), 155-163.

Realon, R.E., Lewallen, J.D., & Wheeler, A.J. (1983). Verbal feedback vs. verbal feedback plus praise: The effects on direct care staffs' training behaviors. *Mental Retardation, 21*, 209-212.

Reitz, A.L., & Hawkins, R.P. (1982). Increasing the attendance of nursing home residents at group recreation activities. *Behavior Therapy, 13*, 283-290.

Repp, A.C., & Deitz, D.E.D. (1979). Improving administrative-related staff behaviors at a state institution. *Mental Retardation, 17*, 185-192.

Spreat, S., Piper, T., Deaton, S., Savoy-Paff, D., Brantner, J., Lipinski, D., Dorsey, M., & Baker-Potts, J.C. (1985). The impact of supervisory feedback on staff and client behavior. *Education and Training of the Mentally Retarded, 20*, 196-203.

Suda, K.T., & Miltenberger, R.G. (1993). Evaluation of staff management strategies to increase positive interactions in a vocational setting. *Behavioral Residential Treatment, 8*, 69-88.

Whyte, R.A., Van Houten, R., & Hunter, W. (1983). The effects of public posting on teachers' performance of supervision duties. *Education and Treatment of Children, 6*, 21-28.

Wilson, P.G., Reid, D.H., & Korabek-Pinkowski, C.A. (1991). Analysis of public verbal feedback as a staff management procedure. *Behavioral Residential Treatment, 6*, 263-277.

Participative Management Strategies

Baldin, S., & Hattersley, J. (1984). Use of self -recording to maintain staff-resident interaction. *Journal of Mental Deficiency Research, 28*, 57-66.

Burg, M.M., Reid, D.H., & Lattimore, J. (1979). Use of a self-recording and supervision program to change institutional staff behavior. *Journal of Applied Behavior Analysis, 12*, 363-375.

Burgio, L.D., Whitman, T.L., & Reid, D.H. (1983). A participative management approach for improving direct-care staff performance in an institutional setting. *Journal of Applied Behavior Analysis, 16*, 37-53.

Doerner, M., Miltenberger, R.G., & Bakken, J. (1989). The effects of staff self-management on positive social interactions in a group home setting. *Behavioral Residential Treatment, 4*, 313-330.

Kissel, R.C., Whitman, T.L., & Reid, D.H. (1983). An institutional staff training and self-management program for developing multiple self-care skills in severely/profoundly retarded individuals. *Journal of Applied Behavior Analysis, 16*, 395-415.

Reid, D.H., Schuh-Wear, C.L., & Brannon, M.E. (1978). Use of a group contingency to decrease staff absenteeim in a state institution. *Behavior Modification, 2*, 251-266.

Richman, G.S., Riordan, M.R., Reiss, M.L., Pyles, D.A.M., & Bailey, J.S. (1988). The effects of self-monitoring and supervisor feedback on staff performance in a residential setting. *Journal of Applied Behavior Analysis, 21*, 401-409.

Shoemaker, J., & Reid, D.H. (1980). Decreasing chronic absenteeism among institutional staff: Effects of a low-cost attendance program. *Journal of Organizational Behavior Management, 2*(4), 317-328.

Determining Acceptable Management Strategies

Davis, J.R., Rawana, E.P., & Capponi, D.R. (1989). Acceptability of behavioral staff management techniques. *Behavioral Residential Treatment, 4,* 23-44.

Davis, J.R., & Russell, R.H. (1990). Behavioral staff management: An analogue study of acceptability and its behavioral correlates. *Behavioral Residential Treatment, 5,* 259-270.

Miltenberger, R.G., Larson, J., Doerner, M., & Orvedal, L. (1992). Assessing the acceptability of staff management procedures to direct care and supervisory staff. *Behavioral Residential Treatment, 7,* 23-34.

Green, C.W., & Reid, D.H. (1991). Reinforcing staff performance in residential facilities: A survey of common managerial practices. *Mental Retardation, 29,* 195-200.

Reid, D.H., & Parsons, M.B. (1995). Comparing choice versus questionnaire measures of acceptability of a staff training procedure. *Journal of Applied Behavior Analysis, 28,* 95-96

General Descriptions of Organizational Behavior Management Strategies for Improving On-The-Job Staff Performance

Arco, L. (1993). A case for researching performance pay in human service management. *Journal of Organizational Behavior Management, 14*(1), 117-136.

Balcazar, F., Hopkins, B.L., & Suarez, Y. (1986). A critical, objective review of performance feedback. *Journal of Organizational Behavior Management, 7*(3/4), 65-89.

Bell, C. & Zemki, R. (1992). How do employees in service jobs find out how they're doing? Good feedback systems. *Training,* 36-44.

Christian, W.P., Hannah, G.T., & Glahn, T.J. (Eds). (1984). *Programming effective human services: Strategies for institutional change and client transition.* New York: Plenum.

Daniels, A.C. (1994). *Bringing out the best in people: How to apply the astonishing power of positive reinforcement.* New York: McGraw-Hill, Inc.

Durand, V.M. (1985). Employee absenteeism: A selective review of antecedents and consequences. *Journal of Organizational Behavior Management, 7*(1/2), 135-167.

Fleming, R.K., & Reile, P.A. (1993). A descriptive analysis of client outcomes associated with staff interventions in developmental disabilities. *Behavioral Residential Treatment, 8,* 29-43.

Ford, J.E. (1980). A classification system for feedback procedures. *Journal of Organizational Behavior Management, 2*(3), 183-191.

Ivancic, M.T., Reid, D.H., Iwata, B.A., Faw, G.D., & Page, T.J. (1981). Evaluating a supervision program for developing and maintaining therapeutic staff-resident interactions during institutional care routines. *Journal of Applied Behavior Analysis, 14,* 95-107.

Prue, D.M., & Fairbank, J.A. (1981). Performance feedback in organizational behavior management: A review. *Journal of Organizational Behavior Management, 3*(1), 1-16.

Quilitch, H.R. (1979). Applied behavior analysis studies for institutional management. In L.A. Hamerlynck (Ed.), *Behavioral systems for the developmentally disabled: II. Institutional, clinic and community environments* (pp. 70-81). New York: Brunner/Mazel.

Reid, D.H., & Parsons, M.B. (1995). *Staff training and management: 1995 Bibliography of organizational behavior management reports in developmental disabilities and related human services.* Morganton, NC: Developmental Disabilities Services Managers, Inc.

Reid, D.H., Parsons, M.B., & Green, C.W. (1989). *Staff management in human services: Behavioral research and application.* Springfield IL: Charles C. Thomas.

Reid, D.H., Parsons, M.B., McCarn, J.E., Green, C.W., Phillips, J.F., & Schepis, M.M. (1985). Providing a more appropriate education for severely handicapped persons: Increasing and validating functional classroom tasks. *Journal of Applied Behavior Analysis, 18*, 289-301.

Reid, D.H., & Whitman, T.L. (1983). Behavioral staff management in institutions: A critical review of effectiveness and acceptability. *Analysis and Intervention in Developmental Disabilities, 3*, 131-149.

Wetzel, R.J., & Hoschoer, R.L. (1984). *Residential teaching communities: Program development and staff training for developmentally disabled persons.* Glenview IL: Scott, Foresman and Company.

INDEX